ENVIRONMENTAL SCIENCE
IN THE PRIMARY CURRICULUM

Jos Elstgeest works at the Regional Pedagogic Centre of Zeeland in the Netherlands, producing teachers' and pupils' materials for primary science. He has worked in Tanzania (1957–73) where he was actively and productively involved in the African Primary Science Programme. He has worked on the UNESCO Maths and Science Teacher Education Project at the University of Lesotho (1973–76). As a member of the Committee for the Teaching of Science of the International Council of Scientific Unions (ICSU/CTS) he has taken part in various activities promoting primary science education and teacher training throughout the world in close co-operation with Wynne Harlen.

Wynne Harlen graduated in physics at Oxford and taught in schools and colleges for a number of years before becoming engaged full-time in research, evaluation and curriculum development for almost twenty years. She gained a PhD at Bristol University through research into evaluation procedures and her first book *Science 5/13: a Formative Evaluation* was published in 1973. She led a team at Reading University which produced three books and audio-visual material for use in teachers' courses for middle and primary school science. During this time she edited *Evaluation and the Teacher's Role* for the Schools Council and contributed to a number of other publications on curriculum evaluation, including *Values and Evaluation* and *Evaluation Roles*. From 1977 to 1984 she was deputy director of the APU science project at King's College, London, before being appointed to the Sidney Jones Chair of Science Education in the University of Liverpool. She published *Assessment in Schools* in 1983, *Teaching and Learning Primary Science* in 1985 and in the same year edited *Primary Science: Taking the Plunge. Developing Primary Science* was published in 1989 and 1990 sees the publication of five further books in primary science to which she has been a major contributor. She has worked for short periods in a number of developing countries and has produced three publications for UNESCO and is principal consultant to Commonwealth Secretariat's project on the development of teachers of primary science. She was a member of the Working Group on the National Curriculum in Science.

ENVIRONMENTAL SCIENCE IN THE PRIMARY CURRICULUM

JOS ELSTGEEST
and WYNNE HARLEN

Paul Chapman Publishing Ltd
144 Liverpool Road
London
N1 1LA

British Library Cataloguing in Publication Data
Elstgeest, Jos
    Environmental science in the primary school.
    1. Elementary school teaching
    I. Title   II. Harlen, Wynne
    372.3'57

ISBN 1-85396-127-2

Typeset by DP Photosetting, Aylesbury, Bucks
Printed and bound by
St Edmundsbury Press, Bury St. Edmunds, Suffolk

CONTENTS

PROLOGUE
CHILDREN AND THEIR ENVIRONMENT

'Environment' is the world around us. It starts with the skin
of our body and reaches out in all directions, in ever
widening circles, until it embraces even the Universe.

Recently, we have departed from the simplicity of this straightforward
meaning. We have dressed the word in many guises and in some contexts it
has become a slogan. Action groups are formed to 'protect' the environment,
and even Green Parties have appeared on the political scene. Our environment is in danger, it is contaminated, it is deteriorating, it must be protected,
it must be controlled. Somebody must do something about it!

But what should be done about it and by whom?

We recognize an imperative to ensure that future generations grow up with
the understanding and attitudes which will reverse the present destructive
influences on the environment. This concern shows itself in curriculum
intentions, such as the National Curriculum for England and Wales which
includes the target:

> Pupils should develop knowledge and understanding of the ways in which human
> activities affect the Earth.

(DES, 1989, p. 12)

Similar statements can be found in other national syllabuses and are more
generally reflected in publications from international bodies, such as the
World Conservation Strategy of the United Nations Environment Programme, the International Union for Conservation of Nature and National
Resources and the World Wildlife Fund (1980).

The instrumental goals of conservation and preservation of the Earth are
not the only reasons for environmental education, however. Indeed, as we are
soon to suggest, they should not be the main ones at the primary school level.
The whole Earth is too large and complicated for children to comprehend.

Children learn about the world only through the small parts of it with which they come into contact, which they *encounter*. It is the nature of this encounter which is so crucial. For if this helps them to see the parts they study as full of fascinating, interesting, challenging, question-provoking and answer-providing materials and opportunities, they will be equipped with skills and enthusiasms to deal with the wide world. If they learn to value, care for and identify with small parts of the environment they will gradually acquire the attitudes for being responsible adults.

Environmental education – what it isn't

Agreeing that Environmental Education is important is one thing, deciding what to do is another. We would delude ourselves if we relied on placing the responsibility we all share onto shoulders upon which it does not belong. Many adults regard the school as the vehicle by which to transfer our own unease and guilt about the welfare of 'the environment', which we prefer to think of as an abstraction instead of as a reality of which we are a part.

Raising the admonishing finger at children is starting at the wrong end. Children do not pollute the environment. They do not spray insecticides, or weedkillers. They do not impregnate the atmosphere with sulphur dioxide. They never hide toluene and benzene in the ground beneath new living areas. They do not defile the surface waters with phosphates and oildumps, or the deep sea with nuclear waste. Yes, they may casually throw away sweet papers and the like but these do not pollute the Earth; they do not even begin to pollute it.

The guilt is ours. Pollution is a problem for adults, caused by adults, and it should be solved by adults. The problem leaves children cold, simply because it is too big. They cannot grasp the nature of it, nor its extent. Naturally, it is easy to talk children into chanting green slogans but this is not 'environmental education'. We should think carefully before (mis)using children in campaigns against practices and policies which adults have failed to control.

For instance, if the success of a 'national tree planting festival' is measured only by the number of schoolchildren taking part, the festival will be of dubious value, if only because it is a 'one-off' event. Children will with equal pleasure shove broomsticks into the ground, as long as it happens during lesson time. The same applies to a communal 'cleaning up day' by school children, as seen not so long ago on TV. Children were shown gleefully picking up orange peels and paper trash from beneath hedges and shrubs, and the beaming Mayor, sidling into the picture, praised the effort as a prime example of active environmental education. Had the dignitory been filmed a week later while walking along the roads of his municipality, he would have changed his tune. A good habit is not established by a single event. The danger lurking in these well-meant, but once-only, exercises does not in the first place threaten our children but, rather, ourselves in our complacency which tends to identify ritual with reality.

We also have to avoid complacency and 'tokenism' by having environmental education on paper, in the shape of a general syllabus or a textbook. Although a good manual, a rich sourcebook, for use by teachers is most welcome, it can never do the work for them and will never replace their own efforts and thinking.

Environmental education – what it is

The general issues of environment are important and we do not wish to negate this when we state that they have to be tackled in primary education through children's interaction with it at their own level, not through handed-down adult concepts. The experience of the environment is unique for every child. Getting to know the environment and learning to understand relationships within it is a very personal experience for the child, who is at the centre of it.

Environmental education begins within the concrete environment of each child, because the child grows up in it, learns from it, belongs to it, depends on it, contributes to it, and even has his own influence on it. Although the environment of each child may be unique, it is not isolated. It is interwoven with and related to, indeed it belongs to, the environment of other children. The school is an important part of the child's development and thus has a natural role in environmental education.

Growing up, learning and gaining insight and wisdom within one's own environment is natural for every child, each in his or her own way, following his or her own aptitudes.

There is a continuous interaction between a child and this environment: the stinging nettle, the shy bird, the sparkling fish, an aunt's purring cat, the shade under the tree in the park, the smell of hay, the greasy softness of a sheep's fleece, and the shells on the beach. Everything is a challenge and demands the child's attention, including fellow humans at home, in the street and at school. It includes the traffic in town, the weather and the seasons, the force of the wind, the speed of cars and the power of machines, and the influences of radio and television. Thousands of impressions beleaguer children, intrude upon them and occupy their minds. Children accommodate themselves to this avalanche, attempt to make sense of it all, and select and create order in this chaos. They establish their own place in it.

These occurrences, part of the natural process of coming to terms with the world, form a basis for environmental education, but are not its essence. Environmental education comes into being when this natural development is consciously and positively influenced, secured, encouraged, enriched and arranged by adults who themselves belong to and are part of the child's own environment and who thus become part of the interaction between the child and his or her environment.

Teachers have a pre-eminent position among these adults in eduction and thus carry an extremely great responsibility. The way teachers act can be very enriching to the children; it can also have the reverse effect – whichever effect, it will certainly be a lifelong one.

Good teaching is a diversified professional activity. It is directed towards helping children to discover their own potential, to develop this further, to build onto it and to have confidence in it.

Good education means that teachers intervene at appropriate times to give their children's learning a new turn, to nudge their activities and attention in a new direction. The need for such intervention is there when a child 'asks' for it, either directly in so many words, or indirectly when he or she obviously seems stuck, or is just freewheeling about. Teachers can create opportunities for investigation, can point out what deserves special attention, and can suggest new topics or build further onto current interests. As they take part in the children's investigations as equal, although somewhat more experienced, partners, they can and should disclose relationships with other objects, events, or earlier experiences which the children would otherwise have missed. In this manner teachers create an atmosphere in which natural inquisitiveness can prosper.

So, as a general aim for environmental education we propose that children are helped to make progress in knowledge, organization, discipline and self-reliance through an active and effective involvement with the world around them.

1
INTRODUCTION: AIMS AND FOCUS

The environment is the whole world, but this vastness cannot be understood by young children. For them the whole world is the small part they have seen of it. But this small part is still enormously rich and varied. The whole of school science can be based on studying the aspects of the world that small children encounter in their daily lives:

- the changes in materials, such as foods when they are cooked;
- the variety of materials in the furniture, in clothing, in buildings, in utensils and tools;
- the predictable and unpredictable changes in the weather, in day length and in vegetation as the year rolls by;
- the forces that are needed to open doors, bounce balls, drive home nails;
- the lights, torches, bells, buzzers and telephones that put electricity and magnetism to work;
- the television, computers, calculators and printers that are part of the commercial, and in many cases the domestic, scene today;
- the sounds from living things, vehicles, musical and non-musical instruments, wanted and unwanted, which surround the child all the time;
- the colours, shadows, reflections, flashing lights, signals and signs which are seen everyday;
- the stars, planets and other things that can be seen in the sky, day and night.

Indeed, science *is* approaching understanding of these events and phenomena.

In this small volume it is not intended to take on this whole range, but only to focus in terms of subject matter on certain parts of the child's environment – those parts which concern *living things and their interrelationships*.

In the terms of the National Curriculum for England and Wales these are the subject of the first four of the attainment targets for knowledge and understanding, relating to:

(1) the variety of life;

(2) processes of life;
(3) genetics and evolution;
(4) human influences on the earth.

In dealing with this subject matter we are, at all times, also developing and using skills and methods of scientific investigation as indicated in the attainment target: Exploration of Science. See p. 59.

Key Points of Emphasis

There are three key concepts guiding our way of dealing with this subject matter relating to living things and their environment in this book:

(1) the importance of the way in which children interact with the content – we call this the *encounter*;
(2) the use of the *school* environment;
(3) the support which *teachers* need to develop the skills and confidence to guide the children's learning through the encounter.

Encounter

We shall say more about this in Chapter 2, most usefully through describing some 'encounters'. For the moment it is enough to say that in an encounter there are questions posed by the child which are answered by that particular object, event, or part of the environment (s)he is studying. An encounter is an interaction, and the invitation to study, to investigate, or to ask further questions, seems to come from the objects themselves: they call for attention. The child's question, or urge to investigate, is a first response to this challenge. Consequently, it is as if a question is asked of the object, and the object itself provides the answer. Are all the pebbles smooth? Coloured? Hard? What does this beetle eat? Does a worm make a hole by itself, or does it use an old one? The answers can be found from the pebbles, the beetle, the worm, by careful observation. For other questions more interaction may be needed, where, for example, a child might change the conditions to see if this brings about a change in something else because he thinks these two things are connected.

In these encounters, the usefulness of the answer depends on the way the question is put and the nature of the interaction. This is another way of saying that what is learned from an activity depends on the *processes* used in collecting and using evidence. We shall say more of this also in Chapter 2. But the following points are relevant here to justify our focus on the living environment.

Much work on living things has traditionally depended on *observation* and *recording*. Emphasis has been on description, labelling and naming, and little else. This has given 'nature study' a bad name.

The way to introduce more science into primary education is not to abandon the study of nature in favour of physical science. Of course the physical and manufactured aspects of the environment should be studied in a balanced science programme, but the natural and living parts of the environment should also be studied *in a scientific way*. It is our intention to illustrate in this book (in Chapter 3) how this can be done and at the same time provide for continuity and progression in learning.

The school environment

There are few schools which don't have a wealth of living things (besides the children) within their boundaries. It requires only a small plot of soil, a few shrubs and trees for there to be seeds and fruits and flowers of various kinds to be studied. Where there are soil and plants there will be a plethora of animals that dig and tunnel, crawl and fly, hide and seek, eat and are eaten, so that children can learn to observe how the behaviour of living things is built into a pattern of survival and procreation. Choose a tree or a shrub, and you choose an interesting living structure which also shelters, feeds or otherwise supports a multitude of other living things. Choose any small area, and make it into a minifield of study. The complexity of interrelationships there is very much reduced to a level that is comprehensible to a child and will thus invariably lead to new insights and to new problems.

Visits outside the school grounds to areas where there is a greater variety of features of the landscape will be easier for some schools to organize than others. Where it is a rare and special event the expedition has to be planned carefully, with the intention of following up with a great deal of further work in the classroom (see pp. 43–48). But the effort is worthwhile in that children extend their skills of investigation, for example by choosing a short transect set out along a piece of string stretched between two points along a line which may pass through small areas of varying appearance: across a path, across a ditch, up a hillside, through a brook, across a dyke, or through a garden. The interrelationships between soils, rocks, plants, animals and other influences such as trampling, exposure or erosion come into focus.

The teacher's role

Although attention is drawn to the motivating power of children's curiosity and their natural instinct to probe, inquire and question, it is not intended here to give the impression that learning in science happens without the help

of the teacher. Quite the contrary. Children's observation and enquiry may be superficial and unsystematic without the questioning, guidance and example of their teacher.

The crucial role of the teacher is subtle and complex. It is not easy. It requires on-the-spot judgement about when to give or withhold information, when to accept and when to challenge children's ideas. It demands decisions to be made about provision of resources, classroom organization, and planning activities so that children's varying ideas and skills can be advanced through their own activity (mental and physical). It seems somewhat overwhelming for someone who has not experienced this kind of teaching and learning and who may feel worried about 'not knowing the science'. In Chapters 4 and 5 we attempt to offer support to all teachers and particularly those who feel lack of confidence in making a start. Finally, in Chapter 6, there is a self-check, a list of questions for a teacher herself to identify the successful and less successful features of her science teaching. Reflection and analysis of our teaching, together with the support of colleagues, will ensure continued progress, as suggested in the Epilogue.

In summary, this book attempts to provide some insight into:

- how the school environment, being an essential part of 'the world of the children' can be exploited as a means to, and a source of experience in, information and learning;
- how in the neighbourhood of every school small bits of environment can be selected which serve as living learning aids so that natural relationships reveal themselves to the children;
- how the learning and practice of a number of process skills, which are the keys to disclosing the riches of the school environment, form the essence, core and centre of the child's science education;
- how we as teachers can enter into the world of the children, where they naturally relate to the things around them, to structure their dialogue and interaction so that it can evolve into genuine science;
- how simple equipment and materials, which can be found in every neighbourhood and are thus always available, can be used within the school to spur the children to learning by themselves and so becoming more self-reliant.

2
CHILDREN'S ENCOUNTERS WITH THEIR ENVIRONMENT: WAYS OF LEARNING AND WAYS OF TEACHING

Let's start by giving two examples which bring out the meaning of the 'encounter' between children and some aspect of their immediate environment.

The first is quoted from Elstgeest (1985) and repeated here because it encapsulates so well this notion of encounter.

> Tiny Niels, beaming, bare and beautiful, crawled on the wet sand. He moved where the sea reaches out for the land, where the ocean barely touches the continent, where the exhausted waves drag themselves up the incline and withdraw or sink into the sand. Whenever this happened in slow and steady rhythm there appeared, all around Niels, tiny holes in the sand which bubbled and boiled with escaping air. These little marvels drew his attention, and with immense concentration he poked his finger in hole after hole, until a fresh wave wiped them all out and created new ones. Then Niels's game would start anew, until an unexpectedly powerful wave of the incoming tide knocked him over and, frightened, he gave up his play and cried.
>
> Witnessing such a simple encounter between child and world, places all our well-learned treatises on child development and on the child's orientation in this world in the shadow. Here on this beach it happened. This was it. And we, adult know-alls, have nothing to add. The bubbling holes invited Niels: 'Come here, look at us, feel and poke.' And Niels did exactly that. He could not talk yet, not a word was exchanged, no question was formulated, but the boy himself was the question, a living query: 'What is this? What does it do? How does it feel?'
>
> (Elstgeest, J., 1985, p. 9)

This anecdote illustrates the challenge of the objects themselves as well as the intensity of the interaction between the child and this phenomenon of nature: between Niels and the bubbling holes. This is learning, but education does not (yet) enter into it. This episode, therefore, is not science education.

In the second example there was a teacher to help the encounter. She and her class were in a meadow:

A little girl examined a dungbeetle. She had turned it over on its back in order to locate its eyes. Suddenly she spotted tiny mites in the softer folds between the harnessed segments of its abdomen. 'I never knew that small animals like insects have parasites too!' she exclaimed enthusiastically to her teacher, and she started to count the mites. In the discussion with her teacher the question arose whether more insects in the meadow would harbour parasites. 'Well go and find out,' replied her teacher and the girl went stomping through the grass chasing up other insects. Soon she caught a green grasshopper which carried bright red louse-like parasites in the folds of its wings. 'Look, Miss,' she proudly showed her catch, 'honestly, I thought only people, dogs and chickens had parasites!'

Her teacher was happy that this child made this relation, because only people, dogs and chickens inhabited her textbook chapters on parasites, but living in the meadow were beetles and grasshoppers, together with their parasites.

(Mary Elstgeest, 1973, p. 5)

In this meadow not only the little girl and her classmates searched around, busying themselves with the insects and their guests. The teacher, too, walked around investigating what dungbeetles and other insects had to tell. At the same time she was watching her children and what they were doing, listening to their tales and reporting, looking at what they wanted to show her, and encouraging them to carry on, allowing them to work by themselves in the meadow.

The girl's question was answered with the suggestion of doing something so that she would find out. She was shown a way to follow, and the answer she obtained satisfied her and made her feel good. Her teacher was as busy with the meadow full of questions and answers as with her searching children. Teaching and learning combined here into the sound science education which enhances orientation.

A third example is to be contrasted with these first two, but may be all too familiar in the experience of children:

A ten year old had been busy in the library corner for at least half an hour on her project on flowers. She had written, 'The flower consists of five parts, "sepals, petals, ovary, pistil and stamens".' This dubious information was backed up by a scarlet felt-tip drawing of something which could be executed in plastic and from which lines sprouted connecting the separate pieces of plastic with the appropriate words. The nodding teacher mumbled approvingly and pinned the product on the noticeboard.

A small tragedy occurred here. Neither in the library corner, nor on the girl's desk was there a real flower to be found. Yet a few flowering plants led a forgotten life on the window sills, while outside there was a profusion of flowers all round the school. The child had been directed to the library corner without a question of her own. Unfortunately, this school library housed little more than a set of know-it-all booklets designed to load the children with informative-looking words; but the real things were silenced in there. A

plastic answer was thrust upon this child to a non-existent question. There
was no interaction whatsoever here, neither between flowers and child, nor
between child and teacher, and even less between teacher and flowers. There
was no encounter; no dialogue; no orientation. There was no teaching; no
learning, no science education.

Science Education

In science education children practise real science. They act, behave and work
like scientists, but at their own level of competence, within the possibilities
and restrictions of their intellectual development and, therefore, very much in
their own way. This, however, is real science, no more, and no less. A scientist
begins from his or her existing ideas or theory derived from previous
experience, and attempts to make sense of new phenomena encountered or to
solve fresh problems. If evidence shows that the theory, or the predictions
based on it, do not fit reality or do not help to solve the problem, then some
change may be made to the theory or an alternative tried. In this way ideas
and theories are modified so that they fit more of the available evidence and
thus become more powerful in aiding understanding of a wider range of
phenomena. But the ideas which are useful are always those which fit the
thinking and the evidence available. These ideas, the scientific knowledge, will
change as thinking and evidence change.

Implied in this view of science is the notion that ideas and theories are
always subject to modification as new evidence comes to hand. Thus,
accepted scientific theories are not regarded as fixed and immovable but,
rather, as the best way of understanding that has so far been found. Moreover,
it should be noted that whether or not a theory if found to fit evidence will
depend in part on the way in which an experimental testing is carried out. The
history of science provides many examples where theories were accepted
when they should have been neglected, or vice versa, because of errors in
procedure and methods rather than the nature of the evidence.

Unfortunately, this is not the view of science that many people have.
Instead, they regard science as the facts and findings; they think of scientific
knowledge as fixed. This is a mistake; we need to see science as the whole
process of coming to understand the world around, as the practice and
processes of looking at the world with an enquiring mind as well as the
concepts and ideas which are the ones most useful at any particular time.

Science does not consist of a mass of formulae. It is the method by which
the creative mind can construct order out of chaos and unity out of variety.
Any formula is the result of such creativity.

Science is not a body of sterile knowledge. It is the fertile skill of acquiring new knowledge, to be added to the body so far recognized, and to keep it alive.

Science is not a string of dogmatic answers. It is a logical and systematic approach to solving problems.

Science is not the ultimate truth. It is the careful search for truth, a search which takes place between the question and its answer.

Science, and consequently science education, is a conscious and intensive activity having its own discipline, its own method of gathering and processing information and its own mode of acquiring knowledge and developing insight. Whoever begins to master this discipline can advance further under his own power. It is a faculty which leads to knowledge and understanding and which emerges from the acquisition of a number of skills: learning skills, problem solving skills and skills which facilitate the process of science.

Ways of Learning

What we have said for scientists holds equally true for children. Basically, science is the same process as that through which toddlers go when they feel, look, touch and taste and generally explore anything that comes within their reach. Thus they begin to adjust themselves to the world in which they were born. It is of little use to lecture a toddler on the hotness of the kitchen stove; each one of us has learned this by painful scientific discovery. Science is the same process as that which young children go through, when they look behind, under or inside things in order to find out how they work or how they are made.

The scientific activities of small children may be a far cry from the systematic orderliness of a research laboratory. None the less, their persistence in exploration and discovery makes them veritable little scientists who are determined to find out. The school should meet this urge and through good science education teach the children orderliness, an insight to relationships and a way of preserving these insights, so that they learn to find out and understand better and more. As a rule the children should be allowed to continue their explorations, but at the same time bring to bear a multitude of experiences provided by or guided by their teacher, as part of their school experience. So that, when children leave school, they will take with them a new faculty: the ability to approach any problem they meet in a logical and scientific way. This skill – and it may well be the most valuable tool the children carry with them – is what makes good science education in the primary school so very important.

Considering the nature of science in this light might necessitate reconsidering the objectives of science education. Instead of teaching about scientific facts, which are the result of the scientific activity of others, it becomes an education through doing science oneself. Instead of trying to remember descriptions of the results of science, it becomes a process of learning how such results are obtained, and doing this for oneself.

Through the exploration and investigation the children are gaining an understanding of the things they encounter. Skills and methods of enquiry cannot be developed or used in a vacuum. The starting point is the existing ideas of the children, which they use in trying to make sense of their new experience and the classroom, outside and in their everyday life. The recognition that children already have ideas about the things around them, and that these ideas play an important part in learning, creates a parallel with the activity of scientists. As we have described on p. 8, scientists use existing ideas as a starting point for these theories and modify them in the light of evidence. Similarly, children (and other learners), through their explorations, are testing and changing their ideas.

This view of learning fits the evidence that research has provided about children's ideas and how they use them to make sense of the world around. It contrasts with the view of the child as having an empty mind into which new knowledge is packed, for it acknowledges the existing ideas which are the child's own. Learning is regarded as the change in these ideas through testing them against evidence in the same way as the scientist tests theories. The change may involve modification or rejection and the adoption of alternatives which fit the evidence better. Whichever it may be, the change is carried out *by the child* and the new ideas become his or her own.

But the ideas emerging will be scientific ones only if the linking of ideas to new experience and the gathering of evidence to test their usefulness are carried out in a scientific way. As children's encounters and interactions become more conscious, more organized, more scientific, so their ideas and real understanding of their environment will grow.

We return, then, to the importance of methods of bringing children and their environment into fruitful interaction. Our focus on process skills at this point is not because they are more important than the growth of conceptual understanding, but because they are fundamental to it. We call them 'process skills' because they are inherent to the scientific process of learning; they can be applied to any content, any subject matter.

Process Skills as Ways of Answering Questions

There are numerous answers to the question: what are science process skills? Generally, they comprise lists including words such as 'observation', 'prediction', 'hypothesizing', 'interpretation', 'communication', 'manipulation', and so on.

Rather than compete with or add to these lists the intention here is to identify the skills which help to answer particular kinds of question. After all, not all process skills are used in every kind of investigation. Which ones can and should be used are related to the question posed.

The questions can be posed by the teacher or by the children. The aim is to encourage children to raise questions for themselves as well as to answer them. The way to encourage this process skill (since raising questions *is* such a skill) is by example; thus at times the questioning is by the teacher with the intention of developing this skill in the children. Questioning is important because one who formulates a question well is well aware of what he or she wants to know. He or she who in addition learns to master a process of investigation and research is bound to find a way towards a solution. The objective of science education is just that: to use clear questioning to lead to answers. How the skills of asking different types of question are related to the skills used and developed in answering them is suggested in the following list.

Questioning skills	*Answering skills*
● *What?* questions	● *Observation*
what is it?	look, watch
what does it do?	feel
what is it made of?	touch
what does it show?	listen, hear
what is happening?	sniff, smell
what do you see, hear, smell?	(taste)
● *How much?* questions	● *Measurement*
how many?	of length, width, height
how heavy?	of area
how long?	of volume
how wide?	of mass
how far?	of temperature
how warm?	● *Counting and*
how . . . what else?	● *Computing*
	of changes
	of growth
	of relations
	of proportions
● *How much more?* questions	● *Making quantitative comparisons*

- *How different?* questions
- *How similar?* questions

- *What happens if?* questions
  These questions can always be answered by action and the children will find some sort of relationship between what they do and what happens as a result
- *How could you . . .?* questions
  These pose problems of finding a way to achieve a certain result or product

- *How?* questions
  how does it come about?
  how does it work?
  how are . . . related?
  How? questions are for thinking as well as for doing. It is often hard, sometimes even impossible, to obtain a fully satisfying answer, and almost always new problems will emerge from whatever answer you get: 'But how, then . . .?'

- *Why?* questions
  There are many kinds of why? questions:
  'why does it happen?' as an expression of wonder and not really of enquiry

- *Making qualitative comparisons and then*
  ordering
  tabulating
  classifying
  graphing
- *Investigation* involving planning to
  change a variable
  control others
  collect relevant data
  order and interpret data
- *Making hypotheses*
- *Making predictions*
- *Testing predictions*
  A hypothesis is a possible explanation of what is needed to produce the result, and leads to a prediction based on it, which can be tested. The testing can involve all the previously mentioned skills
- *Recognizing and using relations associations*
- *Discovering and using patterns*
- *Making abstractions and using them*
- *Reasoning*
  (a) *Induction*, which is possible and valid only on the strength of many observations and experiments.
  (b) *Deduction*, which is reliable only on the basis of valid induction

'why?' meaning for what useful
purpose – it may be possible to
observe this
'why?' meaning what mechanism
brings it about? – this can be the
subject of enquiry
'why?' meaning why are things as
they are? – this is metaphysical
and not open to scientific
enquiry

(Further discussion of questions and questioning can be found in Elstgeest, 1985, and Jelly, 1985.)

To these questioning and answering skills can be added:

- The skills of expressing oneself clearly in spoken word
  in writing
  in sketch or drawing
  in diagram or graph
  in model or action
- the skill of applying one's own resourcefulness and creativity;
- the skill of reading and consulting written sources;
- persistence;
- sociability in co-operative effort;
- readiness to respect the view of others and to reconsider one's own in the light of convincing evidence or reasoning.

Ways of Teaching

Having looked at ways of learning and at the objectives of learning, the next obvious question is how is it all to be achieved? Since the way of learning is different from the traditional (not by rote but by encounter) and the objectives are also different (not facts and figures but process skills and tested ideas), then it would be expected that the way of teaching would be different from the traditional. *How* different is illustrated by a few sample lessons. All three lessons are on the topic of seeds, fondly cherished in all syllabuses and curricula with good reason, for they are wonderful little packages of life, and the guarantee of our survival. Fruits and seeds are present in any environment and always easily available everywhere. They are also full of challenge.

Lesson number one

This example takes us to a rather typical traditional science instruction class. The teacher writes the title of the lesson on the blackboard: 'SEEDS'. Next to this he draws an impeccable diagram of 'The Bean'. The bean is open to reveal its inner parts which, together with its outer parts, form 'the internal and external features' of the bean, carefully labelled as such by the teacher.

Not a single detail is overlooked. Lines connect the parts with the correct words: testa, cotyledons, plumule and radicle. As usual, the teacher finds difficulty in drawing the micropyle, but the appropriate line indicates its approximate location just below the hilum. The function of each part is minutely described, the rather dubious assumption that the micropyle allows water to enter the seed is not excluded.

While reciting this lesson, the teacher writes a neat summary on the blackboard. The last part of this mainly Greek language lesson is devoted to the children writing the summary and copying the diagram into their copybooks.

In the weekly, monthly, or annual test the children can now answer questions such as: 'Name the external and internal features of the bean'; 'What is the function of the micropyle?'; 'What is the radicle?', and so on.

The purpose of this lesson clearly is: to teach about the seed and its parts. The effect of such a lesson can be analysed as follows. The children, more used to eating beans than to having them exposed naked and enlarged on the blackboard, do not get enormously interested in the content of this science lesson. They will duly attempt to learn the difficult words from their notes and to answer the questions in their next test. They are, however, likely to forget, soon and completely, whatever they have learned from this lesson. They will continue to eat their beans with gusto or disdain depending not on the plumule, but on the way they have been cooked.

Lesson number two

This time we witness a teacher who has modified his lesson. For some time the trend has been to move away from the 'talk and chalk' approach depicted in the first lesson as being not a very penetrating way of confronting children with the facts of life. An 'activity method' prevails in this class.

The teacher has soaked a handful of beans overnight in a glass of water in order to soften them up. Each child is given a soaked, soppy bean or two, together with a pin and a hand lens. The diagram on the blackboard now grows gradually as the children pry open their bean with the pin. The actual testa, hilum, cotyledon, plumule and radicle are pointed out by the teacher, and the children compare each part in turn with the developing diagram on the blackboard. They see the real thing. Naturally, the micropyle is elusive in spite of the hand lenses, but squeezing the soppy beans does reveal its presence, and a little imagination added to the lens makes it visible to some. The teacher's running commentary includes the function of each part and, below the diagram on the blackboard, grows the summary to be written into the children's exercise books.

The children in this lesson are much more involved than those in lesson number one. Therefore, it should surprise no one that they remember the parts, and even their Greek names, better. They may even point them out to their parents at the next meal. The purpose of this lesson still is: 'to teach *a b o u t* the seeds and their parts' through the bean.

The likely effect of this lesson is that the children enjoy it more than the chalk-and-talk lesson. They may well score better in the next test, as they are well informed about the bean. Whether they have a deeper insight into the structure and the working of 'seeds' remains to be seen. This lesson is pure instruction and is still far removed from problem-posing science education. It is still encapsuled in the testa of the bean and misses the open-endedness of the following lesson.

Lesson number three

The teacher in charge of this class does not begin by writing on the blackboard, simply because there is nothing to write about yet. He realizes that one lesson period cannot possibly be sufficient for the children to become familiar with seeds, and he is not at all sure, yet, exactly where the activities are going to lead. He does have a plan, but much will depend on the response and the interest of his children. The only thing he is sure of is that, if the children are to study seeds, they will need seeds. Not beans, but seeds. Not one seed, but many seeds. Not two kinds of seeds, but many kinds of seeds and any type of seeds. Not a handful of seeds, but heaps of seeds. So, the first problem to be solved is: how and from where do we obtain seeds? And out they go, in search of many seeds, not to the bean store, but to the fields, to the bush, to the hedges and lanes, to the meadows and the shrubs, to the trees and the grasses.

On their return the children have a large mixture of seeds, pods and fruits, along with many questions and problems, the first of which is how to bring order into chaos. Fruits, pods and seeds are grouped according to features recognized by the children. The bell, ringing too soon after this introductory period, almost restores the chaos when the children scrape their prizes together to store them away for the following science lesson. There is no way of predicting exactly what is going to happen next as, from here, the lesson may develop into various directions.

The greater the variety of collected materials, the more diverse the problems and activities are likely to become:

- Can you find a fruit with only one, with two, with many, with how many seeds?
- How are the seeds contained in the fruit? Side by side? Touching? Separated? Overlapping? Loose or attached?
- How are they attached? Structures and arrangements are studied and compared.
- Who has found the biggest seed? Who has found the smallest? How can we measure seeds?
- Do plants that look alike have similar seed structures? Or do plants that have similar seed structures look alike?
- Do grasses produce fruits and seeds?
- Do you find the same number of seeds in each pod or fruit of the same plant?

A large number of similar pods are arranged on the table or desk according to the number of seeds they contain. Thus a natural histogram can be built up, and new questions can be asked and answered.

There is no end to the possibilities. Finding clues to make a reliable estimate of the number of seeds per tree might become a challenge. The viability of all seeds is questioned.

The development from flower to seed is often traced, since many plants contain fruits at all stages of growth. The travelling structures of seeds catch the interest of many children. The insides of seeds are invariably explored, and the Greek words are simply translated into 'two halves', 'a tiny plant' and 'skin'. And can you find in one seed the parts you observed in another?

At one time or another all get involved in making the seeds grow into plants. Stubborn seeds may ignore the three conditions of germination found in the textbook! To the children these seeds are a real challenge: How do you get them to germinate when you seem to have tried everything?

Many more problems arise. Numerous 'what happens if?' problems are tried out, and the children are busy, noisy, excited and ignorant of Greek words. But they will soon regard themselves as 'seed experts', and with a good reason. They have seen it and they have done it. They have grown seeds on paper, on bricks, on pebbles, on cotton wool, on sponges and in soil. They have grown plants from halves and from quarters of seeds. They have established that the 'tiny plant inside' grows first, and that the 'two halves' help it to grow. They have made hard, stubborn seeds germinate by filing

Root

Stem (stalk)

leaf - leaves

Flower

them, or boiling them, or cracking them, or by just being patient.

Difficult 'why?' questions were broken up into more approachable 'let us see how . . .' questions. Accuracy, persistence and patience have been recognized as necessary virtues of the young scientists. They have learned to be more careful in their predictions, for which they have found ways of verification. They have harrased each other in discussions and they have shared many ideas and much information. In order to find more satisfactory solutions to some of their problems, they had to find better ways of experimentation, and to control variables previously overlooked. In the process they began to realize that seeds do provide answers, but only if they are 'asked' in the right way. Because they did find solutions to their own problems, and did learn on their own, the children have gained much self-confidence.

The test of this lesson is not the weekly, monthly, termly or annual test but, rather, a continuous experience of asking questions and trying to find answers. Intellectual progress is then best evaluated through the children's work showing increasingly effective use of the scientific process skills relevant to their ideas about seeds as living things.

The purpose of this lesson is no longer 'to teach about the seeds and their parts', although the outcome will have this effect. The purpose of this lesson is: 'to encourage the children to pose and to solve their own problems using seeds, and to practise all their scientific skills in doing so'. The seeds have become the teachers; the children have become the talkers and demonstrators; and the teacher has become the listening guide.

The effect of this prolonged lesson is that the children have received training in thinking, learning and scientific problem-solving. They have practised and increased skills and techniques which they can apply to other and further scientific studies, and in the process they have also learned a great deal about seeds.

This third lesson also throws some light on the shifting position of the teacher, who is to create situations which challenge the children: first to identify a question and then to find a way to answer it. Such situations can be created by providing the children with (simple) materials, or by helping them to investigate their natural surroundings. How to select these opportunities, guide the learning, bring about the fruitful encounter of children and things in their environment – these are things which concern us in the remainder of this book.

3
SETTING UP THE ENCOUNTER

Let us first visit a few classes of children and watch how they work in their own environment:

(1) Infants are still at one with their environment. They are totally immersed in it, and seem to belong in it as naturally as the buttercup in the grass, the bird in the bush, and the clouds in the sky.

A class of infants and their teacher ambled along the track of a disused railway where nature had taken over. The place had become a natural reserve, a bountiful piece of wasteland where a great variety of wild vegetation flourished and bloomed. Each pair of children had been given a wooden hoop, normally used in games. The teacher carried a bagful of magnifying glasses, empty jam pots and polythene bags.

They were going to 'work' with 'minifields'. The children were allowed to throw their hoop down, anywhere they liked, thus creating a tiny round minifield for observation: they were to look very carefully for what grew or moved within the bounds of their hoop. In the beginning they made sure to 'catch' at least one dandelion or daisy or any other pretty flower. But later they started the game of 'did-you-get-this-too'. From then on they started to pay real attention to all the plants found within the circle of their hoop, also to those plants which had no flowers at all; and they became interested in shapes and in forms of growth. They even began to tell kinds of grasses apart. They soon began to search for new plants in order to throw their hoops around these and be the first to 'catch' them.

Such a conscious experience cannot but leave an impression on the exploring children, even though they may forget all the names of the plants. Names were not important; they asked for them but were satisfied as soon as they knew that there was a name. They were encouraged to make up their own names for unknown creatures. It was striking to notice how often the names they invented somehow expressed their observations.

The thunderstorm which slowly gathered above their heads in

darkening threat made a great impression. This added the third dimension to their awareness of the environment, for up to then they had been too occupied by the length and width of their minifields. In the nick of time they made it back to the school. From the shelter of the classroom they watched this element of the environment: the slanting rain, the splashing and spattering and the rings and bubbles appearing in the pools that quickly formed outside the windows.

(2) A class of nine and ten year olds were working on wood. They had searched all over the school building for the various uses of wood in the building, framing, decoration and joinery. This exploration connected the many kinds of wood and their properties to specific uses, which was further elaborated upon by a local carpenter who contributed much information with great verve and lively anecdotes.

The children went to the woods to unravel some secrets of living wood hidden in the shrubs and trees. They learned to understand the tell-tale scars which indicate spurts of growth in preceding years, while sawn off stumps told their own story of how wood is made, from the inside.

Their attention was drawn to the dying and rotting wood which lay about abundantly in the woods. They took a lump of decaying wood with them back to the classroom. The treasure hidden in such a mouldering clump is immense. Out of it came shy minibeasts, such as springtails, thread-thin centipedes and surprisingly coloured spiders. When a big piece of bark suddenly tore loose under the exploring hands of two of the children, hundreds of woodlice cascaded across the table, giving rise to shrieks, giggles and shivers. Those who got the creeps could watch from a distance, while the brave ones counted the woodlice and touched them. The teacher told the children to watch carefully what the woodlice would do. After some panicky crawling about, most of the woodlice found a place to hide and were no longer to be seen.

This was a golden opportunity for the teacher. The behaviour of the woodlice provided a wonderful lesson. Realizing that the woodlice had to be housed in order to be studied, she asked: 'Can you think of something which would make the woodlice feel at home?'

Fortunately, nobody had a ready-made answer, and the problem triggered off a useful discussion:

'Where were they to start with?'
'What was it like there? What would it feel like in there?'
'They quietly stayed there all the way while you were carrying that stump.'
'Where are the disturbed woodlice now?'

Their earlier experiences, and the discussion, led the children to an experiment. They made a 'woodlice house' in a basin with moist turf and pieces of loose bark for the woodlice to crawl under. It worked, and confirmed their hypothesis that woodlice like moist, dark and safe places. But the log soon began to dry up, and what happened then is the beginning of another story.

The structure of wood and bark is easily observed and comprehended in such a piece of mouldering wood. The fibrous structure, which is easily prised apart in a waterlogged, rotting chunk of wood, can be clearly recognized in 'proper', dry wood, too. This is also described and graphically represented in the books that the children use and refer to when working with wood.

(3) A school was fortunate to have a farm not too distant from the school. The farmer had 'adopted' the top class for a year to enable the children to follow closely all goings and doings on the farm through a complete yearly cycle. A few times, in different seasons, the children made an excursion to the farm, which also served to boost activity in the classroom afterwards.

On this occasion it was potato planting time, and the farmer's wife sent the children to a vast empty field where the farmer was busy planting potatoes. He did this with the help of a huge dibbling machine which simultaneously planted eight potatoes in deep straight furrows. The machine was drawn by a large tractor which had a roomy glass cabin on top, a kind of popemobile on high wheels, in which the farmer sat while travelling to and fro. At every turn he invited five children on a dibbling trip to the end of the field and back. That was fun, and quite an experience. However, one disadvantage was that the children had to wait a long time before everyone had had a turn. As could be predicted, the waiting crowd became bored and naughty, which was not part of the plan. The bags of seed-potatoes were stacked on a large flat cart while awaiting planting.

Some children borrowed a few handfuls to have a good look at what makes potatoes 'seed-potatoes'. They had 'tiny eyes', and the obvious question was: 'What are these?' There was a point of dispute! One insisted they were roots, another knew that they were called sprouts. 'But what are sprouts?' 'Well, a kind of root.' 'But roots are white.'

The discussion did not get much further until, from another bag, some potatoes were produced which showed sprouts of greater length on which one could recognize small roots emerging and even the pale beginnings of leaves. Now it was easier to understand that these 'eyes' really were the tender beginnings of the new potato plants. These children were ready to start thinking and experimenting in the classroom:

- Can we grow a potato plant out of it?
- Do all the 'eyes' on one potato grow into new plants?
- If not all, how many?
- Can you plant half a potato and still get a new one?
- What if you plant a sprout only?
- How much potato is required to make one 'eye' grow into a plant?

And, of course, other experiments can be performed with sprouting potatoes:

- Keeping the potato in the dark; how long will a sprout grow?
- What happens to the potato itself while the sprout grows?
- Who can grow the longest potato sprout? Would it help if you nip off all the others and keep one growing?

The potato field itself had been prepared and it looked bare and empty; but that was an illusion. Many little plants were actually growing and there were many seedlings of the larger weeds growing along the edges of the field. This provided the opportunity to go and search for at least twenty plants of different species. The children took up this challenge and in no time discovered ten, but then it started to become more difficult. 'Who can still find another plant which we do not have yet?' This game compelled the children to look more carefully and to take more notice of details, so they could establish similarities and differences with more conviction. They did not reach the number of twenty distinct species. No matter, because they had observed the seventeen they did find very well indeed.

These examples, of course, are only snapshots, tiny episodes, to be followed in spirit and attitude, rather than to be copied. They tell their own tale, and clarify what follows. Copying is not possible; for instance, you cannot order a thunderstorm to break during the science lesson! Even if you could, you would miss the spontaneity of the right question at the right time. Rather, it is necessary to learn to be alert in the use of the school environment; teacher as well as children acquire this alertness only by practising it in their own environment. We shall come to this presently.

What has Your School Environment to Offer?

There are as many school environments as there are schools. Each one of us is surrounded by a unique environment, and that is the one we must become familiar with.

What follows can be read in the comfort of your easy chair – and by all means, do read it at leisure. But if you want to use it with effect, then you must step outside and walk around and explore your school environment, all the while considering how you can make the most of the possibilities it offers. A teacher can carry out this exploration alone but it is preferable to do so with colleagues – ideally the whole teaching team. It is imperative to coordinate the work of the children in different classes who will be drawing on the school environment as a source of learning. Because the children in different groups differ in age, interests and abilities, each teacher will approach the environment in his or her particular way.

Infants, i.e. the youngest children (up to the age of seven), want to see, watch and touch everything that can be seen, watched or touched. They like to do everything they can think of with whatever is available, as long as it lives, or blooms, or moves about, or otherwise amuses and fascinates. They watch and peep, they sniff and smell, they touch and feel, experience every possible sensation, and chatter incessantly about everything they do.

Lower juniors (seven to nineish) demand many experiences, but require these to be more ordered and directed because they like to learn how things are related, or how things are fixed together; how they work. They love to take things to pieces and to put them together again, the former enterprise being usually more successful than the latter. They like doing 'What happens if . . .' experiments and they enjoy practising (newly acquired) skills, from sharply searching to correctly ordering, from not spilling when pouring liquid to accurate measuring, from good observation to careful manipulation.

Somewhat older children, (ten, eleven and twelve year olds) are able and willing to concentrate on more specific problems. They can speculate about the possible outcome of an action or experiment. They can build up a hypothesis and put it to the test in an experiment in which variables are recognized, considered and appropriately controlled or manipulated. Nevertheless, just as for the younger children, the first encounter must be spent making acquaintance, getting to know, exploring and experiencing, before they take their next, really scientific, step forward.

These comments refer to the general development of children, given that they have had sustained experience of working in the way proposed here. Where this is not the case – and in *any* case for individuals, who rarely fit the average picture – it is important to match the experience to the children. To do this it is necessary to pick up information about the children's existing skills and ideas, which can be done using the methods for formative assessment that we describe later (p. 51–55).

Look around wisely

Keeping some insight into your children's capabilities and knowledge at the back of your mind, explore the possibilities and opportunities in your school surroundings to motivate your children towards sound science:

(1) Which landscape or elements of landscape do you find around your school?

A landscape is a piece of earth, small or large, that can be recognized as a complex whole. There are many kinds and many sizes. We think of the large rural, agrarian, mountainous, forested or prairie-type land- scapes, not forgetting seascapes. Landscapes may be wild like moors, or cultured like a park. But there are small landscapes, too. Think of your own playground and its surrounding shrubbery as a landscape. Or take a footpath and its verge, or a piece of wasteland; the village green, or town square, or a front garden; a hill side, a brook, a bank or a copse, a lawn or a flowerbed. These are all landscapes, each forming a complex entity, each recognizable by its own particular characteristics.

On a still smaller scale, look for minilandscapes, such as an overgrown wall, a mouldered, mossy stump of treetrunk, a hollow tree such as an ancient pollard willow. Anything might raise questions about what grows and flourishes (or not), about what is happening or what has recently happened, about what has been erected, constructed or put in order. Don't just look for green or bloom; non-living things also speak a language. Notice, for instance, the pattern of the bricks in the buildings or the paving slabs in the streets. Since our focus here *is* the living environment we won't pursue the avenues opened up by non-living materials in great detail, but they should not be ignored when working with children.

(2) Don't only search at ground level. Look up! A tree, a hedge, a shrub in the shrubbery already takes the eye upward, but let it go further; there is so much to explore above eye level. There are colours and shapes and constructions of many kinds; kites fly, as do birds, aeroplanes, flies and other winged creatures. The sky, with its clouds and rainbows stretches above, and the whole world is filled with sounds and fragrances. Feel changes in temperature as the winds veer in new directions; watch how the sun seems to move, and how the moon changes place and face.

(3) If your school is near the coast, there may be a beach nearby where the high water mark is full of treasure. Or a sandy plain where the wind moulds wave patterns, or where the rains leave little river systems and patterns of erosion.

(4) If your school has a farm nearby, this can be an enormously rich

experience and it is very worthwhile to cultivate the friendship and interest of the farmer so that children can visit and investigate. What grows in the fields? Did the farmer intend all of it to grow in the field? Does only grass grow in the meadows? What else grows there? If it is a dairy farm, what animals are kept? How? Where? What animals does the farmer keep? Cattle? Sheep? Goats? Are there more animals belonging to the farm? Pigs? Fowl? Turkeys? Rabbits? Dogs? Cats? Which other animals walk, fly, scurry, and sneak about the farm? Does the farmer want those? And . . .? One can keep asking and looking and finding out on a farm.

(5) If there is an interesting industry, suitably small and safe, it will be valuable for children to visit and to observe how things are manufactured, or investigate the raw materials that are delivered, stored and used. Visits to industry offer many other opportunities for education in other areas of the curriculum (see Smith, 1988).

(6) If houses are being built in the neighbourhood, make use of this whenever you can. Not only are there many skilled people working together (which can be observed from a safe distance), but many problems of space and construction are actually being solved right there! It isn't difficult to obtain (by showing interest) samples of the interesting materials to be found there: cement, bricks, wood, metals, plastics and so on, for the children to investigate in the classroom.

(7) Is there a garage, car-works, repairshop, bus station, airport or railway station with a shunting yard?

(8) Are there other interesting structures such as a swing bridge, or a lift bridge, a sluice or a lock, a pier or a ferry-boat installation? Is there a belfry or a carrillion?

In the search for potential in the environment, don't ignore tourist guides or local and national societies which exist to study, protect and preserve the environment. These often produce posters, pamphlets and brochures, and sometimes produce other valuable learning materials to buy or borrow, such as books, films and videotapes. Information and ideas also come from science teachers' associations (e.g. Association for Science Education and School Natural Science Society, see p. 75).

One area may be richer than another, but every area is richer than you expect at first sight. The important questions are:

- What do we have?
- What can I do with all this?
- How do I create order in this astounding assortment?

- How do I select, and what, to bring to the attention of my children? How do I set them to work on it?
- How can I help my children to profit most from it? How can my children perform good science with it at their own level and in their own way, asking their own questions and finding their own answers?

On the following pages there are suggestions and directions (not rules) which are intended to be extended and enlarged as you wish, and which you should adapt and improve to fit your own specific circumstances, according to your own interests, creativity and resourcefulness. These suggestions are intended to complement the many other good ideas which you may find in other helpful texts and books (see Further Reading, p. 74).

Take stock of what is already available within the school library for books have an important role particularly when they send the children to explore the real things in nature, and when nature sends the children back to the books to find out more.

Working in the School Surroundings

A walk

One is inclined to think that the walk is the simplest activity to be undertaken in the school surroundings. Beware the familiarity, however. Remember that the children are walking on their home ground, where familiar things around them have different associations for them than for the teacher. It is, after all, their neighbourhood, their playground, and walking around makes them feel released from the restrictions of the classroom; they think that they have seen everything. So a walk should not be just a walk; it must cover new ground or provide a new challenge on familiar ground. Otherwise it is not worthwhile.

This is not so where infants are concerned. Their radius is still rather small, and thus any walk may present something new. As a rule they delight in it and if they pass through a familiar neighbourhood they inform each other of all they know about the houses, the neighbours, the gardens and the shops. Whenever possible, however, find for this age group also a slightly less familiar route where there is plenty to see and experience, such as through a wood, around a duckpond, past a farmyard full of chickens or machines, past a saw mill full of sounds, past pretty front gardens full of flowers, or whatever you find worth while. Stop frequently to encourage the children to observe (look, listen, feel, smell) and to talk freely.

A walk with older and wiser children should, of course, be less free and leisurely. Careful preparation should put children on the alert for the challenges they will face. The walk may resemble a 'nature trail' where at certain places carefully formulated problems are to be solved. The solution to these problems must be 'hidden' on the spot, so that good observation and sound reasoning is called for. Structures, as well as living creatures, can be the object of observation and study. Avoid the role of tourist guide who names things and talks incessantly about them until nobody listens any more. By all means, give information which is important and which the objects themselves do not provide, but only where this leads to a question or clarifies a question. What this means is illustrated by the following example.

> In country lanes in spring there is a lavish display of wild chervil or cow parsley (*anthriscus sylvestris*). It is interesting to take children to a spot where it grows in uninhibited abundance. In this setting we can consider: where the balance is between telling children something about cow parsley and letting the plants themselves answer the children's questions.

In preparation you can point out to the children what the wild chervil (cow parsley) looks like, the names it is given and where it prefers to grow. Now they can go and search for it. You might also explain how it survives winter underground by forming rhizomes which spring up and sprout in the early warmth of spring. They might want to dig up a plant to see the rhizome and what you mean by your description of it. Such introductions are by no means exhaustive, but leave plenty of questions unanswered, so there is enough scope to 'ask the cow parsley itself'. The attention being thus focused, the children are ready to tackle such questions as the following for themselves:

- Where in this area do you find most cow parsley plants?
- Where are the tallest plants? Where the smallest?
- Are the longer stalks also the thicker ones?
- How many flowers do you find on one stem?
- Would you call the whole umbel one flower? Or is each flowerlet a complete flower?
- How many flowerlets do you find in one umbel?
- Can you find seeds?
- Are there insects which seem to visit the flowers? What do they look like? Do they visit other kinds of flowers nearby, too?
- What other plants grow among the cow parsley plants?
- What is the structure of the plant? How do its parts fit together? (It is interesting to make cross-sections at intervals from bottom to top; through the roots, the stem, the nodes, the leafstalks, the flowerstalks, the flowerheads.)
- Can you find other plants with hollow stems?
- Make a flute out of a cow parsley stem by cutting a sizeable tube, one end open, the other end closed and cut just below a node. Then about half way

down the tube make a lengthwise incision on one side of some 10–12 centimetres. Now blow forcefully through the open end.

- How does it make sound?
- Can you change the tone?
- Does the pitch depend on the thickness of the tube, or on its length? Or on the length of the slit?
- When the flute is being played, what is felt by passing a finger along the incision?

Of course, nobody would ask all these questions at the same time. You can probably devise quite different questions and problems. The ones you use must depend on the interests of the children, but it is important to have considered potentially fruitful (i.e. leading to enquiry) questions. Within this preparation you can avoid 'do-you-see?' and other questions with 'yes' and 'no' answers only.

Whenever you go for a walk, ensure that the things you find important really do 'speak' to the children, and that the children actively 'listen'. Give them clear instructions and well-formulated problems which can be solved or the spot. Create – for it is an act of intellectual creation – answerable questions where the objects themselves will provide the answers, as long as the children look and do.

The ideas suggested in relation to cow parsley can be mirrored in question about:

> clouds in the sky, the colours and movements on the surface of water, the sound in the air, the churning of waves, the folds and cracks in the rocks, the crystals in stone, fossils and landscapes, structures of human ingenuity such as machinery and vehicles of transport, railway bridges, and hoisting-cranes, and other feats of engineering such as the working of the automatic controls at a railway crossing

A word of warning: outings on a grand scale, requiring elaborate work – and question-sheets, run the risk of becoming once-but-never-more events. Avoid this situation by keeping your walks short in time, simple in scope unsophisticated in content and direct in assignment. Prepare the work with care, and prepare the children for their task. In this way you ward off perils, tiredness, boredom, unwanted escapades, searches for toilets and plying the children with 'did-you-knows'. A good and instructive science walk can almost always be continued by, or followed up by, work in the classroom with the collected materials or data. These walks can thus become an integral part of your teaching routine and plans.

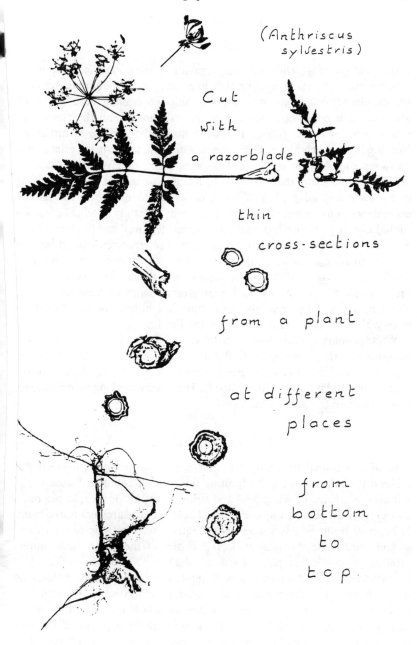

(Anthriscus sylvestris)

Cut
with
a razorblade

thin

cross-sections

from a plant

at different
places

from
bottom
to
top.

Working on a Minifield

Relevance

Living and growing, while we often regard it as commonplace, is quite an extraordinary process. Anything that lives and grows is confined to some specific place and depends on the local conditions prevailing there: on the soil and what it is composed of, on weather and climate and the amount of exposure to, or shelter from, sunshine, rain, wind and other disturbances. Nothing lives entirely alone. There are the eaters and there are the eaten; some creatures encroach on others and displace them, or give them shade or provide protection. Others move, lift, trample or nibble. Every surviving living thing has adapted itself to some extent to conditions of mutual dependence in its own community. That is why the study of fellow creatures should not stop at their 'external and internal features' or appearance, and even less at the names we have given them. The creatures around become more fascinating if studied in the wider context of their community, however small, where every creature acquires its own singular significance. Moreover, the concept of 'community' will gain greater depth of meaning for the children, which is a prerequisite for mature insight into the wider relationships within our larger environment of the Earth.

While primary children are not yet able to come to grips with the global environment, they can cope with the small environments of minifields and begin to conceive the relationships prevailing within them, along with the connections and influences from outside. This is why working with minifields is so important in science education.

What is a minifield

A minifield is a small fragment of ground, clearly marked to a convenient size to keep it comprehensible; by limiting the area, attention is focused. The minifield is created by using pegs and string, or sticks, or slats, to peg out a convenient area of, say, a square metre. The exact measurement is irrelevant. A hoop or frame of any shape will do equally well, as long as an area of suitable size is clearly delineated. The choice of the field is not entirely arbitrary; it should be a piece of ground which, for some reason of another, looks interesting. General interest is the guide when children are first learning to use minifields; later the area of interest may be decided by a specific problem. Look for interesting areas within the school grounds or garden or nearby along the verge of the road, along banks, in the fields, under the trees or by the hedge in a park. Even a slightly neglected path or pavement may show a variety of growth, often small 'bonsai' brothers of plants found in the vicinity.

Preparation for minifield work has to involve a discussion that is mainly concerned with raising questions which the investigations will try to answer and instructions about procedure. Arrange for the children to work in groups (three is a good number), give them directions for reaching, choosing and marking out their minifield, and provide ideas for mapping its contents. If all this is new to the children, a worksheet may be used initially, but make sure that this incorporates the requirement for *them* to suggest questions, such as those set out below, as well as your set questions. When children become used to this they can take greater responsibility for choosing the site and what they investigate in it. After clearly marking a minifield, the first thing is to look carefully at what is there. What lies there? What sits there? What stands there? What hangs there? What grows there? What walks there? What crawls there? What lives there?

At first the children just explore, without worrying about the names of plants and animals, simply looking for what is there. If there is a real need for a name, and you do not know the 'proper' one, make up a temporary one, based on something about the creature. What is important in the first place is that children look very carefully at what they find. Study the nature of what lives there, how things live and lie together, and how these things relate to one another. The 'what do you find there?' questions (p. 11) help, as do the questions below, but if the children get too dependent on questions asked by their teacher, they forget to approach their minifield, or other field study, with an inquiring mind. It is our task to teach the children to ask their own questions. None the less, ask questions yourself to provide examples but make sure that your children know that these questions never exclude their own.

Some initial questions

- How many different kinds, or species, of plants can you distinguish in the minifield? Can you count how many? How does each kind grow? Alone? In twos? In clumps? In tufts? In tussocks? In bundles? In groups? Are they connected? Above or below the ground?
- What distinct parts of the plants can be distinguished? How do they fit together?
- Which kinds (species) of plants occur most? Which one seems to dominate? Are they most in number? Can you count them? Try it. Or is it because of its size that one plant dominates a minifield? Are there any kinds of plants of which you can find only one?

Because it is difficult to take it all in at once, and even harder to remember everything afterwards, it is important to make a map of the minifield, for recording your findings. Divide the map into four, so forming a grid in which objects can be placed with precision. Children might make a rough map in the field, while investigating, and later draw it out more carefully in the classroom, adding anything that is relevant, such as samples taken and dried, or figures counted, or further information gleaned from reference books.

Attention should extend beyond the plants. Collect data about the other inhabitants of the minifield, such as insects and other minibeasts, or their tracks, or what they have left behind.

What is the soil like? What colour does it have? What is it composed of? What other things are mixed with it? Is it dry, wet, fine, coarse, granular, gritty, loose, friable or sticky? Children can pick up some soil on a wet finger and smear it on their map, showing its colour, or trap some soil under sellotape.

Turn the children's attention to relations between the things you find in their minifield. Do plants crowd each other out? How? Are things being eaten by a grasshopper, for instance, or a caterpillar? Are there any spiders' webs suspended from taller plants? Can family relationships be identified, such as separate shoots sprouting from runners above, or rhizomes below, the ground? Are there parents and children together: seedlings, larvae, or even eggs (which spiders sometimes carry around).

What interferes with the minifield? Do people or larger animals trample or otherwise disturb it by cutting, picking, mowing, hoeing, weeding or digging? Are animals or insects eating each other? Chasing each other? Trapping each other?

Are there objects lying about, such as seeds, fruits, stones, plastic bags, drinks cans? Can you find out where they came from? Are they in the way of the objects growing there? How do they obstruct, or protect, these objects?

Once you are busy, many further questions will occur to you, and to the children. Questions should be welcomed. See if the minifield can provide the answers on the spot. If not, no harm is done, for unsolved problems are part of the product of the encounter and lay the path to further investigation.

Organization for Progression

Working with minifields is not a goal in itself, but it is a powerful learning aid, which deserves to be employed whenever the opportunity to do so presents itself. The same can be said about transects, which we consider a little later. The learning experience will change as the children progress in their study of the environment. The nature of the change is illustrated in the two examples below which illustrate how working with minifields might be organized with children of different ages or experience.

For upper infants or lower juniors the work is planned to refine skills of observing and recording. By preserving their observations on a map or in a report of some kind, the groups can compare and co-ordinate what they have done. If they worked in different places, or made minifield maps of the same place at different seasons, they can make meaningful comparisons. In other words, they learn that their records can speak for themselves.

Hopefully, this work helps to develop the children's understanding of the mutual dependence of living things and of their dependence on other influences, too. For the time being, however, it is a matter of observing well, noticing detail, and recording appropriately and clearly.

The teacher's lesson notes may be set out as follows:

Plants in the minifield

Children to work in groups. Each group needs: 4 slats, 2 plastic bags, 1 trowel, 2 sheets of paper, 1 handlens.

To go to the meadow behind the church.

Problem: is only grass growing in the meadow?

Organization:	• Form groups of three children per group. • Each group collects its things. • We go all at the same time. • In the meadow we spread out. Each group makes a square of slats and starts working according to the instructions on the worksheet.
Questions:	• How many different kinds of plants can you find within your square? • Describe two other plants growing among the grass. • Make a map of the minifield which shows where the different plants grow. • Report on anything special or unusual within your minifield.
Rounding off:	After twenty minutes: back to the classroom; complete maps and records. (Compare and discuss results.)

For older children we slowly introduce an element of reasoning about how things in a community influence each other. Ideas relating to such concepts as 'dominance', 'competition', 'struggle for life', 'habitat' or 'community' may be introduced or developed, not by verbal explanation but by trying to trace the relationships.

The teacher's lesson notes might indicate the following:

The study of minifields in the meadow behind the church

Discussion: Every plant strives for a good place in the sun. It so happens that they are often in each other's way. This is called C O M P E T I T I O N. Do you know any examples?

Each group is to make a minifield and address the questions raised through observation.

Questions:
- How do the different kinds of plants occurring there manage to get and to keep their place in the sun?
- Which plants grow taller?
- Which ones creep among the others?
- Which plants make a 'tapestry' excluding others?
- Which twine and twist around others in order to find their way upward towards the sun?
- Look under the flat spread leaves of a dandelion or a daisy. What grows underneath?
- If there is an 'empty' spot, what flourishes there?
- What happens to the plant around which a climbing plant is entwined?
- Make up further questions by yourself and try to find answers to them.

Conclusion: After twenty minutes back to class. Each group reports to the others about their findings and interpretations.

Look carefully, too, at what sits underneath, and at the bottom, of your minifield ...

... and do not forget to look at what hangs above it

In other words, study your minifield with great care, but not in isolation!

Working on a Transect

Types of transect

A transect is a cross-section: a line which cuts across everything in its path. To make one, stretch a taut length of string across several metres of ground, and proceed to investigate the strip extending 15 cm on either side of the line. (For children who find difficulty in limiting themselves to the narrow strip, lay out two parallel strings 30 cm apart.) The transect looks like an elongated minifield, and indeed it can be used as such, but it also has some characteristics (and advantages) of its own. Basically, the idea is to list whatever grows and lives inside this narrow strip, but also to watch how things behave, how differences succeed one another, and what mutual relationships can be discovered. Findings should be recorded accurately, again preferably on some kind of map, or spatial representation.

One difference between a transect and a minifield is that a transect almost always contains some transition: a visible change of appearance. A transect may pass from the road, across its verge to under the hedgerow, or it may stretch across a ditch, a stream, a pond, or a hill top, thus including (part of) opposite sides (e.g. north and south). It could run from inside a pond or a ditch, up its side and across the footpath, or it may begin in a wheat field and end on the tractor trail.

Another difference is that the transect represents a larger territory. The reason for making it such a narrow tract is that one does not become lost in a plethora of details. A class of children can cover a large area by making a number of transects, running parallel, or in a continuous long line. If children are well versed in this way of looking at things (and they need a great deal of practice in some less ambitious activity first) they may obtain a fair impression of the nature of a rather complex landscape, such as a coastal region, or a forest. Studying a 'long stretch transect' which runs a considerable distance over varying terrain makes an interesting co-operative class activity. For instance, the transect may start in the woods, pass through brushwood and across a road, run through a hedge and ditch to half way into a field or meadow. Each group of children is assigned four or five metres of its length. When they join up their maps, making one long record of about the length of the school corridor, this is guaranteed to become an attractive and intriguing piece of work.

Recording a Transect Study

As in the case of the minifield, the results of the investigation of a transect ought to be comprehensively recorded and communicated. Again, a good way is to make a map with the perspective of a bird's eye view (for a minifield) or, in the above case, of a side view of the cross-section. The idea of mapping is to indicate spatial relationships and proportions of length. The 'map' or 'side view' then serves as a basis for any further information to be communicated in the form of description, drawing or sketch, or (preserved) specimens. Long rolls of paper can be used for recording: old newsprint or leftover rolls of wallpaper are useful; but you can also join sheets of paper in one long strip. Find a convenient scale, so that all descriptions, photographs, samples, sketches, names, smears of soil, prints, rubbings, objects, feathers, skeletons, castings, leaves, etc., can be arranged to advantage in their proper position. This can result in a colourful and varied product containing an astonishing amount of information.

To facilitate representation of scale, the string should be clearly marked using either colour, knots of firmly attached labels to indicate metres (or any other convenient unit of length). Specimens taken from the transect can be collected in plastic bags which are equally clearly labelled as pertaining to specific 'metres of string'.

The use of transects is particularly suited to acquainting the children with features of a more complicated character while avoiding confusion through irrelevant details.

Focusing questions

In studying a minifield almost all the details are of interest. When investigating a transect, however, many details are overlooked in favour of attention to those features which indicate broader interrelationships. For instance, in a minifield the type of plant is important, while in a transect it is the type of vegetation that you are looking for. This shift of emphasis is the teacher's responsibility and should be incorporated without confusing the children. In a minifield they scrutinize all creatures and objects within its limits, whereas in tackling a larger area with the help of transects such details would become too numerous and burdensome. The nature of the teacher's questioning should divert the children's attention from the individual details to the broader aspects of objects seen together.

The concept of 'vegetation' develops through looking at plants growing together. The question of 'dominance' becomes relevant now: 'Which plant is most conspicuous?' 'Which creature seems to dominate the others?' It may be a type of plant which is bigger than others. It may be a tree which overshadows the rest. It may be a kind of plant which is present in greater numbers. It may be a grazing animal. It may be a man, sowing, pruning, weeding, trampling, cultivating, planting, mowing or reaping. Talk about this with the children but always in connection with what they see and investigate. Observation, investigation and reflection will support the formation and development of these more complex ideas and concepts.

Where a distinct transition occurs, questions such as the following help the children to look, to notice details and to relate one thing with the other.

(1) Where the vegetation suddenly changes, what other changes are there, such as differences in the soil, more shadow, more sunshine, more, or less, moisture?
(2) Is there a hedge, a wall, a big tree, a ditch, a brook nearby? What changes are associated with its presence?
(3) Look for signs of disturbance by traffic, trampling or other activity.
(4) Look for changes in ground slope. Where does it become steep, or flatten out?
(5) Look for changes at the surface. Is it becoming more rocky, strewn with rubbish, or dug over by insects, worms or other creatures?

Enquiries like these require observation but are within the reach and capacity of children. The process of making these enquiries and the resulting evidence provided help children to develop a mature conception and a higher level of abstraction than do ideas of interrelations between living things. As they gain experience the children confirm, adapt and refine conceptions made earlier. Such work, however simply performed, provides the first steps towards, and awareness of, the environment, along with a consciousness of control that we (personally as well as communally) have over objects in nature, i.e. over our environment.

Span a string across the area or feature you wish to investigate. Limit your observations to a maximum of 20 cm., or less, on both sides of the string.

For beginning children it is good to use a colourful ribbon. I often stretch two ribbons, about 30 cm. apart running parallel.

) tie knots in the string at intervals of one meter. This makes it much easier to locate features accurately and to map them correctly afterwards.

Working on a Larger Area

The activities connected with minifields and transects can, as a rule, take place in the vicinity of the school and within a measurable time. Initially, these activities have a twofold purpose: (1) to master some techniques and operational skills useful in field study and environmental science; and (2) to benefit from the information thus obtained. The skills include careful observation and accurate recording, in written or map form. The benefits to the children include, along with some knowledge of plants and animals, a constantly expanding insight into relationships, connections, interdependence and interactions among living things and between themselves and the elements in their surroundings, through which such complex ideas as 'habitat', 'community', 'environment' eventually acquire form and meaning.

As well as the small-scale investigations, however, it is a good idea for children to occasionally investigate an area of a larger scale, i.e. a larger whole. This requires more time, good organization, thorough preparation (by teachers as well as by the children) and a sound programme of work or activities. You might well need the assistance of a few helpers, such as parents. It is good for the children to 'tackle something big'; it encourages them to co-operate and it can provide direction to, and content and materials for, much fascinating work, first in the field and later in the classroom.

It is wise to choose some distinct 'natural region' for this purpose, such as a forest, a moor or a coastal plain. Schools fortunate enough to have residential field centres available to them will be able to take advantage of the range of very different landscapes to which these provide access. Generally, though, one must be content with a more modest choice since the study area must be readily accessible and not too distant from the school: a particular dale or down, a wood, a park, a marsh, a mudflat, a hillside, a railway embankment, a copse, a piece of wasteground, a glen or a beach.

Each visit to the larger area requires a greater amount of time: a whole afternoon at least. It does not matter that a bigger excursion like this can only take place on rare occasions, as long as it is carried out well and some result ensues. This result could take the form of increased interest of the children, new problems to work on and plenty of scope and material for further work in the classroom.

The following may serve as a basis for a programme, although not everything suggested here will apply in every circumstance:

(1) Collect the materials which could be of use on the excursion:
   - writing and sketching implements;
   - paper (of course);
   - bags or boxes (plastic) in which to collect and carry objects
   - implements for digging, cutting, scratching, striking, sticking, poking, pushing and pricking;
   - instruments for measurement and close observation, such as measuring tapes, calipers, perhaps a spring balance, handlenses and binoculars;
   - whatever else you consider may be useful.

(2) On arrival, before any investigations are proposed, let the working groups of children walk round the area. Tell them to find a place which catches their interest, which they like, and allow them to have a good look around. Then they should:
   - try to describe the place, or sketch it, or both;
   - write down their first impressions;

- characterize the place in a few sentences.

They may try doing this in more than one place before making their choice. Give them the option of choosing a small place: a clearing in a wood, a pond, a copse, a hedge, or a larger place such as a lane, the side of a ditch, the bed of a brook, an area dominated by tall trees, the edge of a wood, a field; even the area as a whole.

It will probably be necessary to help the children with this task, not only to distinguish the wood from the trees, but also with the description of the area of their choice. It is somehow difficult for children to give a global description without getting lost in details. Before sending them off, you could use the gathering place as an example, and discuss a possible description of it as an example: 'This is a shady spot under high trees with dense foliage; on the ground there are a lot of dried sticks and dead wood. Little else grows here.'

(3) Start investigating, guided by such questions as the following. Now is the time to notice details, to work on a smaller scale, to watch for small creatures. Everyone will need to squat or kneel down, crawl about or lie flat; some may need to climb a tree (!) Carefully probing and digging will increase the wealth of what is there to observe:

- What is the first thing that strikes you?
- What is growing there? What is there that walks, crawls, creeps, wriggles, slithers, squirms, glides, hovers, hums, zooms, drones, flutters, flies, or swims about?
- Where exactly are particular things growing or moving about? Pay attention to the immediate surroundings of these things. Where, and on what, for instance, does the fungus thrive, the moss grow, or the seedling sprout?
- Where is that beetle scurrying to? And where is that worm slithering? What is the centipede hiding under? What is green with moss or lichen? On which side?
- What creatures have made a home there? Look carefully for nests, holes, burrows, hollows, lairs, webs and whatever you find that has been spun, glued, stuck, woven, joined together, or otherwise built or constructed.
- What signs are present of creatures (which?) living there? Have they been spinning, building, digging, scratching, walking, eating, nibbling, dropping, fighting, shedding hairs or feathers or whole skins, peeling, or fighting?
- What other tracks or remains can you find there?
- Try to discover relationships, or infer relationships between things and occurrences, for instance bird droppings on the ground and a nest in

the tree; mould and rot; food remains and food eaten; sounds and the soundmaker; track and track maker.

- Look up, look down, in front of you, behind you, and underneath; dig and probe, and sniff and feel.
- And listen . . . and listen again. What do you hear that you were not aware of hearing before?

(4) After allowing sufficient time to look round and to follow suggestions such as those given above, the focus of attention should be narrowed. Try to bring some order to the observations, and help the children to choose a 'speciality'. This involves concentration on some detail which they find particularly interesting. It will be the focus of all the further work in the field and in the classroom and the basis of the report of the study. Some may choose as a group, others as individuals.

(5) If the work could involve collecting things and taking them back with you for further study, make sure thought is given to whether this can be done without causing pain or damage. What cannot be taken away (to exhibit) can always be sketched, described, or photographed. When things *are* taken, the children should note carefully where they have been taken from.

(6) No doubt teacher and children will encounter problems, riddles, puzzling things. That's splendid! Problems should not be avoided since they lead to the most interesting and motivated work. Try to formulate clearly any problem that arises, taking in all the potentially helpful information from the surroundings. Then it can probably be followed up later.

(7) Finally everyone returns with notes, findings, data, problems, surprises and collections. Immediately ensure care of living materials which were brought back.

Naturally, an extensive out-of-doors activity such as this requires thorough preparation which should include making binding arrangements with the children. Decide beforehand on the composition of the working groups. Make yourself thoroughly familiar with the working area, and limit it so that you can keep an eye on all the independent working groups. Adapt ideas from those given above and your own to suit the area chosen. Prepare a sheet of such ideas for the children but make it clear that they should add their own, deviate and take opportunities to study the unexpected.

The excursion should be rounded off with an exchange of discussion in class where the groups exchange their experiences. It could be left there, but it is more likely that the field work will lead to continued work on all the problems that have been gathered and on the materials which the children collected. There will probably be an embarrassing richness of possible follow-

Some more Minibeast-in-environment Questions.

Do the same kinds of minibeasts live and thrive in different places? For instance: flowerbeds, railway embankments, farmland, lawn, road verge, hedgerow, garden, hill top, down, dale, ditch, wood, brook, pool, pond, meadow?

-Or is there something in different places which is the same?

- Or, what is particular to different places where
a) the same minibeasts live?
b) different minibeasts live?

Is it moist or dry? Watery? light or dark? warm? cool? Overgrown? Open? Screened? Bare?

How wet is wet?
How warm is warm?
How light is light?

How do you measure all this?

Do little beasts, that live in a similar (or in the same) environment, have anything in common? Colour? Shape? Eyes? Skin? Breathing organs? Legs?

•Do little animals change if their environment changes? How?

• What do they do if and when you yourself change their environment?

Does the place tell you anything about the (small) animal(s) that live(s) there?

Does the animal (its structure) tell you anything about its natural environment?

Observing any minibeast: what characteristics make it suited to the place where it lives? What characteristics of the place make it a suitable environment for particular minibeasts?

Do they live solitary? In pairs? In groups? Or in multitudes? Who eats whom?

up work and this requires careful planning in order to prevent chaos or disappointment. It helps if the children could be brought into the decision-making: What is really worth pursuing further in class? Are we able to do it? Have we time for it? What additional materials or equipment would we need for a proper investigation? Do we have them? Finally, what shall we select? How are we going to carry it out?

In your planning, allow lesson time for the follow-up, even if you don't know beforehand exactly what it will be. Work which comes from real questions asked in the real environment are at the heart of environmental education and should not be neglected. We thus round off this chapter with a brief discussion of facilities within the classroom.

Working with the Environment in the Classroom
Materials and equipment

While some outdoor work is essential to environmental science education, it is not necessary for most lessons to be out of doors. Some outdoor observations, such as keeping a regular track of certain changes, or growth or the weather, take only a matter of minutes. The weather, although a focus of study itself, will often interfere with plans to go out for long periods of fieldwork. It is thus important to consider what can be done in the classroom.

Some equipment and materials are needed and it is best if these are versatile and usable in several ways. Much can be collected by the teachers with the addition of objects that children can bring in. It is possible to find from the neighbourhood biological materials, such as plants and (small) animals, feathers and hair, fur and scales, flowers and leaves, weeds and spices, fruits and seeds, tubers and bulbs, corms and tendrils, owls' pellets and shells, mosses and algae, rocks and soils, and also things to prick and pry, to keep and store, to stick and dry, to sprinkle and pour. Problems on germination and growing, problems on form and function, problems on feeding and housing, problems on reaction and behaviour, can all be taken up in the classroom, provided there are the appropriate objects to work with. What is 'appropriate' here are those things which form part of the children's world. Children must handle things, for they think with their hands, and if their hands are kept still there is good reason for worry about their work and thought processes.

Perhaps your school is very limited in resources from the immediate environment: lifeless concrete, bricks and mortar, infertile and barren land with little challenge to offer. Although it is hardly ever as bad as this, it is possible that you may have to look a little farther afield, or invoke the help of others. It may require effort to find or create the resources necessary to buy the equipment, which is not cheap, such as lenses, microscopes, measuring devices, calipers, balances, magnets, mirrors, batteries and bulbs, string, sellotape, and so forth. The result repays this effort, for the classroom becomes a richer learning environment.

Another obvious way of enriching the children's learning environment is to provide pictures, illustrations, photographs, paintings and reproductions and, above all, good books full of clear illustrations, comprehensible texts and stories. Film and video are media which take the children outside their direct surroundings, or into those parts of it which they would not reach by themselves. Everything which brings distant features to within the children's experience, is a welcome enrichment.

We should ensure, however, that these media, especially books, 'converse' with the children. A good book directs the children back to the reality of the projects that they are engaged in, or it satisfies a curiosity aroused by some real experience. There are, unfortunately, books, and other media, that serve only to close issues by an 'I-shall-tell-you-the-right-answer-to-give' attitude. It is advisable to keep these out of the classroom. Instead, provide a variety of books – reference books, storybooks, find-out-books – which support the child's dialogue with the things he has encountered by sharpening insight and by co-ordinating relationships which would otherwise escape attention. Surround yourself and your children with plenty of books of these kinds and fill your class with materials, 'objects' and opportunities to work. Also, provide invitations to work, such as work cards or problem sheets that are tailored to the learning at hand. Provide children with uninhibited access to all these materials because they need them to learn from, as much as they need a teacher.

Discussion

Often, whole-class discussions take place towards the end of a lesson, when the teacher invites the children to report their individual group work and describe their investigations, what they found and what new problems they have encountered.

A similar class discussion, or conversation, can be held at the beginning of the next lesson, or activity period, when it does not interrupt the children's work. Then you pick up the important threads where you left off. Such discussion, involving all the children in the class, and most usefully conducted with them sitting around in a circle, often leads to new or renewed interests, to examination of each other's work and exchange of ideas about it, and to guesses of hypotheses and fresh plans for further investigation. The teacher's contributions to these conversations are of equal value to those of the children, but could easily be seen to weigh heavier, so it is important not to let this extra weight dominate the discussion and so smother free exchange.

Class conversations of this kind offer the teacher an opportunity, almost unobtrusively, to make corrections, to challenge the children's reasoning, to give them further motivation, to dot the i's and to cross the t's, and to help the pupils to distinguish between what is relevant and what is not. The children themselves also do this. They correct one another effectively, and indicate what they want or need by continuously asking – of the teacher or each other – for clear exposition or explanation. Because each child speaks from his or her own experience and investigation, each knows what s/he is talking about, and the others know it too.

A second kind of discussion, equally important, is that between the teacher and a small group or an individual child. These discussions have to be approached carefully if they are to be fruitful. When children are not yet ready to communicate, they should be left alone. Don't blunder in with: 'Well? Do you know it now?' or: 'Have you finished . . .?' Watch and listen first to judge whether or where an intervention is welcome. Sometimes children ask you to intervene. They may do this directly or by some less obvious indication, such as a puzzled frown or sitting still, with or without a thoughtful expression, because they may be stuck and not know how to carry on. At other times you may become aware of their puzzling through listening to their chatting. Follow this up by entering their conversation with a neutral remark such as: 'I wonder what you are so busy with', after which it will soon be evident whether they want your assistance, or not, yet.

Providing Information and Asking Questions

The kind of science education advocated in these pages is a long way from the kind which involves chalk and talk and closed questions from the teacher. Now it is the pupil who asks questions in the first place and the plant, animal or object being studied provides the answer, i.e. does the talking. The teacher listens, points out, indicates, explains, admonishes, assigns and encourages so that the children learn to pose their problems clearly and work out how to find a solution. The teacher's role also includes answering children's requests, some of which will be for information. Appropriate bits of information are often very useful; they may fill gaps where the required information may not be readily available to the children, or is difficult to find. Sometimes the information provided (by word or book) may indicate less obvious relationships, thus linking related concepts to form a fresh idea or new point of view. At other times the information concerns a correct name or technical term, which cannot be deduced from the nature of the things themselves.

Don't be afraid to provide children with information of this kind, but try to provide it when needed or when it is useful; when it is appropriate to what the children are doing and busy with; when it leads to new interests. The information should clarify some problem, or underpin it, help the children to connect certain matters into a relationship which they are capable of understanding, but which they would overlook without your intervention. Make it a rule that you do not tell them what they can easily find for themselves.

Often, the clear definition and introduction of a question or problem provides enough information to lead the children forward in their investigative activity. That is why the tasks which you give your children, by word of mouth or in written form, must include questions.

Of course, these questions do not call for an immediate verbal answer. Make sure first that the children realize that your kind of questioning is intended to make them think and work, and that you do not want an immediate answer. The type of question which is intended is a **do-question**. It is a problem, distinctly posed, that the children can handle; it invites them to DO something, to observe something well or, once more, to design an experiment in order to verify some prediction or hypothesis, to reason out something. A good do-question is contextualized so that the answer can be found from the immediate surroundings. For instance, if you want to ask the children how many legs a woodlouse has, then they must have a woodlouse at hand. Don't ask 'where do woodlice live?' unless you are in a place where they do live and can easily be found. Don't ask how fast a plant on the windowsill grows, if the children have no opportunity to measure and record it daily. A good question can always lead to a satisfactory answer, although this answer need not always be complete and final. Almost always the solution to one problem will give rise to another. It will often happen that a problem cannot be solved all at once and that a simple solution is not available. This does not matter at all, for the impulse for further investigation is wanting to know.

It is our intention that the children themselves become skillful in disciplined and systematic questioning and that it becomes a habit. Recall the kinds of questions outlined in p. 11–12, which run parallel to the corresponding skills and abilities that would enable children to tackle these problems. This outline may be useful when you formulate questions to set children working, and can also be borne in mind when in spontaneous conversation with children. Practise this kind of questioning and reflect on it, in order to get it at your fingertips or, rather, at the tip of your tongue. Deliberately try to get out of the habit of asking questions which are based on factual knowledge and which trap the children.

There are books and publications and guides which help you to ask the right question at the right time (e.g. Elstgeest, 1985). It is important to remember, however, that the book may contain the right question, but only you can judge the right time! The questions which you put and the questions posed by the children in lively encounter and interaction are always better than problems on paper.

Children's notes and recording

Notebooks, folders or files constitute a form of communication between the pupils themselves or between pupil and teacher. They complement communication in discussion and in conversation.

While not everything needs to be recorded, graphic communication in any form lends greater coherence and permanence to the children's work. As a manifestation of mental activity, it may contain components which one cannot express in spoken words, such as situation sketches, drawings, tables, graphs or diagrams, maps and mathematical formulae, or symbols. A file or folder for collecting their own graphic work should be part of the children's equipment. Children should be helped to make and use it well, for it is an extension of their memory and a reference to their thinking.

Before they are able to write, children can already give expression to what is taking shape in their minds by drawing, sketching or painting. Learning to write increases the possibilities. Gradually, the teacher introduces such special techniques as ordering numbers, tabulating data, drawing graphs and using diagrams, so that recording findings gradually becomes a matter of course in the children's activities. If the children are given sufficient time and encouragement to master this skill by continuous practice, then each entry in the notebook or folder will become a reference book for later use.

Children rarely keep records without the encouragement of the teacher. But as soon as they realize that their written work is an essential part of their activities and they find it is useful, then they adopt and accept it quite naturally. Moreover, children love having something to show to others, something that is their own.

When recording, graphically or in words, has been accepted as a regular means of aiding communications, with oneself and with others, then it works like a mirror. The children's ideas are reflected in various ways and are of great value to the teacher who wishes to take account of children's existing ideas and skills in his or her planning (see the next chapter). Avoid discouraging this communication by 'marking' it or elaborately correcting it in red pencil! Good work books are honest and genuine, and they show what children have thought about and how; what they have observed and how;

what they have noticed, what they have understood, and where their interests lie. The workbooks indicate those children who can work independently, as well as those who need help and the areas in which they need it.

Workbooks also indicate where children become confused or get lost. The mistakes and understandings which come to light in a child's honest recording show where help and assistance is needed. Comments on the children's written work are best confined to helpful suggestions, and encouraging, if critical, remarks should be made at the appropriate place in the workbook. Alternatively, the response to the written work can be an informed discussion with the individual child.

Where a warm relationship has been established between the teacher and his or her children, and where the children feel uninhibited in expressing themselves, even in their recording, they will talk and converse freely with their teacher, accept sound criticism, and listen with eagerness and confidence. They are eager to communicate with the teacher, through their spoken and written work, and therefore they will readily accept comments which are made in a positive form and which they can see as relevant.

4
ASSESSING THE ENCOUNTER

What do we Mean by Assessment?

Assessment is a word which carries with it a range of associations, mainly unpleasant and to do with teaching. Gradually, however, it is being understood in a more positive light, as a word which embraces a wide range of ways of gathering information about children and which is, and always has been, an integral part of teaching. Assessment involves gathering information which is then compared with some expectation and results in a judgement as to how the child meets that expectation. The process can be extremely informal and hardly noticed or, as in a formal standardized test, carried out according to conscious, rigid, procedures.

Many aspects of regular teaching can be seen as assessment within the broad meaning adopted here. When a teacher responds to what a child says or does in normal classroom transactions, there will be a smile or a frown, a verbal pat on the back, an admonition or a written comment. These are spontaneous reactions but nevertheless they do involve the teacher in judging what the child did or produced against some expectation. The judgement, i.e. that the child's action does or does not meet that expectation, leads to the teacher's reaction. In such circumstances the expectation is likely to be relevant to that particular child – 'child-referenced' – and the same behaviour from another child might produce a different reaction because the expectation is different. The purpose of such assessment is to provide immediate feedback to the child and the differing 'standards' of judgement do not matter.

In other cases it is desirable to use the same basis for assessing all the children, perhaps so that comparisons can be made, but, more particularly, so that appropriate learning activities can be provided. In the case of standardized tests, this basis is 'the norm' or the average for the age group (norm-referenced assessment). The results of such tests indicate how a child compares with others but not what he or she can and cannot do; the tests have little diagnostic function. Thus 'criterion-referenced' assessment is gaining ground because it *does* provide information which indicates what children have achieved and, therefore, what the next step might be in their learning. This is the kind of assessment we discuss here and will exemplify after a few words about reasons and methods.

Why Assess?

Again we can find many and various reasons for assessment. The reasons resulting in children being labelled, streamed or classified are those which have given assessment a negative image. There is far too much evidence of these judgments leading to attitudes and actions which are self-confirmatory. It is important to keep these dangers in mind whenever and whatever assessment is involved.

The purpose of assessment which we focus on here is essentially that of helping learning; indeed it is a part of the teaching–learning process. The notion of 'starting from where children are' is now well established in sound primary school practice; assessment, as we regard it here, is about finding 'where they are' so that the way of teaching and learning, which started from there can be a reality and not just a slogan. We are primarily concerned with gathering information which is used to help children's progress. Many teachers succeed in gathering information about some aspects of learning or about *some* children (usually the ones who achieve well above, and those who are well below, the others). By discussing the process of assessment, making explicit what it involves and bringing the whole process to a greater degree of consciousness we aim to help teachers become more systematic, comprehensive, and rigorous in their assessment.

Another set of purposes of assessment must not be ignored. These involve providing information about the children's progress to all who have a part in it – the children themselves, their parents, the teachers into whose care the children pass at the end of a year and the headteacher, who should be aware of the progress of all the children in the school. It is not necessary to carry out extra assessment to meet these needs, for the information collected and used by the teacher can be summarized in ways that are appropriate for these audiences. However, the need for the teacher to keep detailed and complete records of the progress of each child is emphasized.

Ways of Assessing

This is not the place to give a catalogue of methods of assessment which can be used for various purposes. Instead we focus on what is feasible and useful for the prime purpose that we are considering here – for the teacher to assist children's learning. Assessment for this purpose has to be an integral part of teaching and learning. We shall not, therefore, discuss tests, either written or practical, standardized or otherwise. Rather, we focus on the information that regular learning activities provide and how this can be used. Not only is this the only *practical* approach, so that teachers and children are not undertaking extra activities purely for assessment purposes, it is also the most *valid* approach, since it is in the context of normal activities that children are truly showing what they can do. A contrived activity or question, posed to them simply for assessment, will not necessarily engage their interest and intellectual capacities.

There are two sources of information for teachers' assessment:

(1) what children do or say;
(2) what children write, make, draw or set up.

The essential difference between these sources is their permanence. Information from the first source is of the moment and cannot (without a tape or video-recording) be replayed. Information from the second can be stored, pored over, compared with later products and evaluated by persons not present at the time of the creation.

The steps involved in collecting, judging and using relevant information from these sources are the same for each, namely:

(1) knowning what information to look (or listen) for;
(2) gathering the information;
(3) comparing it with criteria which helps to inform about the children's progress;
(4) using the result to help the children.

It is only in the second step, of gathering information, that the source makes a difference. Clearly, information from actions and speech has to be gathered by observation (which includes listening) at the time, or not at all. By the same token it is impossible to gather such information about more than one child at a time and a systematic approach is required to ensure that each child has his or her turn as the focus of observation.

Rather than continue the discussion in general terms it is probably more helpful to provide an example. For this purpose we consider the two minifield lessons whose outline plans were given on pp. 33 and 34.

Procedures for assessing progress: example 1

The first step, of knowing what information to look for, is indicated by the aims of the lesson (p. 33) (in this case conveyed in the three following questions):

(1) to observe different kinds of plants;
(2) to describe features of plants;
(3) to record, make a map and, later, report.

The second step, of gathering information, requires decisions about how to do this, and then doing it. Some information comes from perusing the children's reports, but for young children, as we are considering here, reports are unlikely to convey the richness of their interaction with the material. Much information must be gathered by observing the interaction. In twenty minutes it will not be possible to gather information about all the children, so it is best to select about five children as the foci of observation in this lesson. In later sessions, other children will be selected as foci. The children should remain totally unaware that they are being chosen; indeed it should not be obvious in the teacher's actions and attention, for (s)he should interact normally with all the children. The difference is that the teacher will make mental (or actual) notes of the selected five, guided by a list of questions, such as the following (the S indicates a skill):

Did the child:

S1. make at least one relevant observation (e.g. find two plants that were different)?
S2. describe an object clearly enough for it to be identified by someone else (e.g. the most frequently occurring plant)?
S3. use a simple instrument to aid observation (e.g. a hand lens);
S4. make any kind of record during the practical work (e.g. draw a map, however rough)?
S5. produce an appropriate report on the work (e.g. a 'tidied' map on which items were correctly identified)?
S6. take part in discussions with others?

Note that:

(1) Included in this list are items which refer to work in the classroom and during discussion, so the observations continue and, indeed, involve looking at the children's products (their maps and reports).
(2) The items here have been expressed in general terms and 'translated' into the specific activity in mind in the examples given in parentheses. The general list is most useful for, clearly, one does not want a separate list for each lesson. At first it is necessary to make the translation but after a while the general form can be used across all subject matter.
(3) It is easy to see how these items relate to the statements of attainment of the National Curriculum (for Science Attainment Target 1). The

observations proposed here can thus be incorporated into the general record of formative evaluation for each child.

(4) The questions not only direct observation to certain aspects of behaviour but are also expressed as criteria for use in making the assessment.

The list of criteria given above concerns science skills only (indicated by the prefix S), because these were the expressed aims of the lesson. At the same time, the purpose of studying 'in the field' is to help children develop their ideas about living things. Thus the following items relating to their *understanding* (U) might well be added:

Did the child:

U1. recognize the plants and small creatures they have been studying as living things?

U2. know that the living things they have been studying have certain needs in order to stay alive?

U3. understand and show evidence in their actions of how to treat living things with care?

U4. know that some materials decay, at various rates, while others do not?

U5. sort living things according to observable similarities and differences?

U6. know that living things share the basic life processes?

U7. recognize the influence of human and other activity in parts of the environment?

In the list there is a hierarchy (indicated by 'levels' in the National Curriculum) and we might not expect young children to achieve more than U4.

Information for assessing against these criteria would come chiefly from discussing the children's ideas with them, to some extent from looking at their written reports and records and also from observation (of how they handled the creatures they found).

The third step in assessment, of comparing the information about children with the criteria, is relatively simple in theory, but extremely difficult in practice! In theory, it is a matter of deciding whether the information gathered meets the criteria. Since the items in the lists given above have been expressed as criteria, it means that the assessment is a matter of deciding 'yes' or 'no' to each question. In practice, of course, there is never clean cut evidence for making the decisions. Generally the evidence is insufficient, fragmentary, often contradictory. What does one do with such real but messy information?

The thought which saves the situation is to remember the purpose of the assessment, which is *not* to label the children but, rather to help their progress. Step 4 (in the list on p. 51) is the important one and if the information helps this step to be taken then the main purpose has been served. Often equivocal information is the most useful for the fourth step. If a child can do something in one context but not in another, this gives a clue about the sort of support s(he) needs. What is different about the situation in which achievement occurs from that in which it does not? We will take this matter of the use of information a little further later, after turning to the second minifield lesson.

Procedures for assessing progress: example 2

In this lesson the aims of the lesson (inferred again from the questions) were:

- to observe the plants in relation to each other;
- to notice patterns and relationships in the different ways the plants grow;
- to propose hypotheses to explain findings and as bases for predictions;
- to record findings;
- to raise questions;
- to use the notion of competition in trying to explain observations;
- to develop ideas about variety and variation in plants.

The same approach as used in example 1 can be again employed with older children in mind. A list of 'what to look for', based on general criteria, is suggested below. The items on the list are used to focus the teacher's observation when watching and listening in the field and when conducting discussions and looking at what the children produce and report back in the classroom.

The numbering of the items in the following list indicate a continuity with the lists used for the younger children. The application in practice is as before, with a focus at different times on different children so that, over time, information is gathered systematically about all the children.

As before (see p. 52) the prefix S refers to a skill and U to understanding. Did the child:

S7.   make at least two relevant observations (e.g. of a plant's behaviour having been affected by another plant's presence)?

S8.   make any measurements or quantify observations (e.g. of height or growth of plants)?

S9.   use instruments appropriately to observe and measure (e.g. hand lens, ruler, thermometer)?

S10. notice patterns or regularities in relationships (for instance, about where certain plants grew taller than usual)?

S11. propose conclusions consistent with evidence?

S12. propose hypotheses to explain findings?

S13. raise further investigable questions?
S14. record findings at the time?
S15. describe (orally or in writing) the sequence, main events and results of the enquiry?

U8. recognize similarities and differences between broad groups of plants?
U9. know about the process of decay and its role in the maintenance of life?
U10. know the cycles of some of the living things they have studied?
U11. recognize an association between the conditions in a locality and the different species of plants and animals living there?
U12. understand the operation of competition and the predator–prey relationship.

Using the Results of Assessment

The results of these lists, based on information from the children's actions and products, indicate the extent to which each child is progressing in relation to the aims of the study of their environment. Many lessons have the same overall aims and so the fact that some will be assessed when working in a minifield in the meadow behind the church, whereas others will be involved in investigating a somewhat different area, does not matter. We must keep an eye on the overall aims relating to children's understanding of, and skills in exploring, their natural environment, not the specific facts, names and information they pick up on the way.

How do we use the information that assessment provides about where children are in their progress? Certainly *not* only by ticking off an item in a record book. It is important to keep records – if only to ensure that we have gathered information about all the children in all relevant aspects – but the purpose is to help the children's learning in direct and conscious ways. The following lists some situations in which teachers can use the information. They are in no particular order:

- If a child is not noticing features which are relevant to the building up ideas about the environment, it may be necessary to sharpen the focus of his or her observation. For a while, rather less open questions may be required. Not just 'What do you notice about the dandelions?' but 'What do you notice about the way the dandelion leaves grow?'
- When children don't respond to challenges posed by 'Why?' or 'How could you . . .?' questions, as shown by failure to propose hypotheses, try 'What happens if . . .?' questions instead (p. 12).
- Talk to a child who has not responded as expected to a task in order to find out what s(he) thought the task was. Consider what the child did in relation

to the perceived task (probably more effective than you thought) and then try to take the activity forward into the direction originally intended.

- Pay particular attention to the child's vocabulary when discussing his or her work. Ask for examples of words which you suspect may be used idiosyncratically and introduce an agreed word where there appears to be a need for it. (For example, one girl called all seeds 'beans' because she had only ever known the bean to be grown from seed. Cress was a bean for her so she needed the word 'seed' to avoid such misunderstanding.)

- Of course, discuss achievement in positive terms but in doing so reinforce those aspects that you aim to develop. For example, rather than 'that's a very good drawing', say 'that drawing shows very good observation of details of . . . and helps me to see where the . . . and . . . were found.'

- Draw the children with less well-defined ideas into a group discussion with others so that they have to explain and try to justify their ideas.

- Use information about children's ideas (which may be logical in terms of their own experiences) but not consistent with the views of others to create opportunities for them to test and challenge their ideas. For example, if children say that seeds grow best in the light (or dark) get them to plan and carry out an investigation which will test the influence of light.

- In many cases, particularly for older children a teacher can talk explicitly with a child about what has been learned and what there is to learn. 'What do you know about . . .?' 'What would we need to do to find out more?'

- Reflect on the way the children are forming their ideas and challenge, not the idea, but the way it has been arrived at. Ask for evidence. Do they think the evidence is 'fair'? What other interpretations could there be? Why did they choose the one they did? Could they think of better ways of testing an idea? Would other conclusions fit the evidence better?

We are beginning to come full circle, to describing how to arrange for children to engage physically and mentally with objects in their environment. This is the objective – assessment helps to focus on those encounters in which learning can take place and sharpens this focus for each individual child.

5
GIVING ENVIRONMENTAL SCIENCE A PLACE IN THE SCHOOL PROGRAMME

Here we attempt to bring into sharper focus those main points which must be addressed when implementing environmental science. Our keynote has been *encounter*, the bringing together of children and their school environment, which is usually also the environment in which the children live. Whether living and growing objects are represented only on a small scale in scanty patches along the sidewalks of an urban area, or are abundantly present in the luxuriant verdure of the open countryside, it is in these places that the children become aware of the interdependence of earth and soil, plants and animals and people and themselves, and thus begin to unravel the complexity of their environment.

From this encounter emerges the awareness of *coherence*. The coherence of living (and non-living) nature manifests itself in numerous ways. Every small piece provides a unique example of how it reveals its own particular aspect. Even within the confines of a square metre of ground, pegged out to form a minifield, one finds coherence in diversity, and evidence of competition and dominance. This is more obvious in the survey of a transect which covers a larger stretch of ground and can be still more readily grasped by engaging the children in a concerted effort of investigating and comparing notes, in a more extended area such as a wood, a moor, a meadow, a farmer's field, or an embankment. In a well-organized field study the children learn not only to distinguish between different types of populations or habitats, but also learn how to look, how to observe, to compare and to register. Gradually they learn to recognize and to classify the characteristics of living communities by gaining insight in patterns of cohabitation, of cause and effect, of competition and of dominance, and thus they can appraise the habitability of a particular milieu.

Making provision for this learning now is considered under three headings: planning, resources and classroom practice.

Planning

The aim of planning is to match up learning opportunities which the study of the environment provides with the learning experiences which are desired or required. The Programme of Study of the National Curriculum (DES, 1989) indicates that children aged five to seven years:

> should be encouraged to develop their investigative skills and understanding of science in the context of explorations and investigations largely of the 'Do . . .', 'Describe which . . .' and 'Find a way to . . .' type, involving problems with obvious key variables which can be solved using a qualitative approach and which are set within everyday experience of children.

These activities should:

- involve children and their teachers in promoting ideas and seeking solutions;
- promote at first hand the exploration of objects and events;
- encourage an appreciation of the need for safe and careful action;
- encourage the sorting, grouping and describing of objects and events in their immediate environment, using their senses and noting similarities and differences;
- increasingly encourage the development of non-standard, for example, hand-spans, and simple standard measuring skills;
- develop an understanding of the purposes of recording results and so encourage systematic recording, using appropriate methods, including block graphs and frequency charts;
- encourage the interpretation of results;
- develop reporting skills, ideally by talking, but also by other means, as appropriate.

> (DES, 1989, p. 65)

and while using and developing these skills:

> Children should have opportunities both to observe at first hand and to use books, stories, pictures, charts and videos to find out about a variety of animal and plant life. Over a period of time children should take responsibility for the care of living things, maintaining their welfare by knowing about their needs and understanding the care required . . . They should become aware of the variety of other life-forms . . . This study should be by direct observation where appropriate and through stories, books, videos and pictures.

> Children should collect, and find similarities and differences in, a variety of everyday materials, natural and manufactured, including cooking ingredients, rocks, air, water and other liquids.

> Children should collect, and find differences and similarities in, natural materials found in their locality, including rocks and soil. They should compare samples with those represented or described at second hand. They should observe and record the changes in the weather and relate these to their everyday activities.

> (ibid, p. 66)

For older children of seven to eleven years a rather more demanding list of skills is suggested:

Children should be encouraged to develop their investigative skills and their understanding of science in activities which:
- promote the raising and answering of questions;
- encourage a working understanding of safety and care;
- are set within the everyday experience of children and provide opportunities to explore with increasing precision, where appropriate;
- build on their existing practical skills within a given framework;
- require the deployment of an increasingly systematic approach involving the identification and manipulation of obvious key variables.

These activities should:

- involve variables to be controlled in the development of a 'fair test';
- involve problems which may be solved qualitatively, but which increasingly allow for some quantification of the variables involved;
- encourage the formation of testable hypotheses;
- develop skills of using equipment and measurement, encouraging children to make decisions about when, what and how to measure;
- encourage the systematic listing and recording of data, for example, in frequency tables and bar charts;
- encourage the searching for patterns in data;
- encourage the interpretation of data, and evaluation against the demands of the problem;
- encourage the development of written and/or oral reporting skills, as appropriate;
- encourage the use of a limited technical vocabulary in communicating findings and ideas.

(ibid, p. 68)

And that these investigative skills should be developed and used while the children

explore and investigate at least two different localities and the ways in which plants and animals are suited to their location. They should explore some ways in which plant and animal behaviour and life cycles are influenced by environmental conditions and seasonal and daily changes and by predator–prey relationships. Using secondary sources and, if possible, specimens, they should explore the range of past life-forms preserved as fossils. They should have the opportunity to develop skills in identifying locally occurring species of plants and animals and marking these against keys, using observable structural features of organisms. They should do this at first hand and through a range of sources chosen by the teacher, with the opportunities to develop increasing independence in the use of these sources. They should develop an awareness and understanding of the necessity for sensitive collection and care of living things used as the subject of any study of the environment.

Children should investigate some aspects of feeding, support, movement and behaviour in relation to themselves and other animals ... They should investigate the effects of physical factors on the rate of plant growth, for example, light intensity, temperatures and the amount of fertiliser.

Children should investigate and measure the similarities and differences between themselves, accessible plants and animals and their fossil counterparts. The study should be extended to cover extinct life-forms and to include basic ideas about genetic and environmental causes. In this study they should give attention to the welfare and protection of living material.

Children should study aspects of their local environment which have been affected by human activity. These may include, for example, farming, industry, sewage disposal, mining or quarrying. Where possible this should be by first-hand observation, but secondary sources may need to be used where there are considerations of safety. They should observe and record the significant features of the process; the range and origins of any raw materials; waste disposal procedures, decay processes and the usefulness of any product(s).

Children should work with a number of different everyday materials grouping them according to their characteristics, similarities and differences.

(ibid, p. 69)

It hardly needs pointing out that the types of activities and approaches described in earlier chapters provide ample opportunities for these experiences. However, the fact that this is the case in theory does not make it so in your particular case. What does your particular environment provide? How can it be studied by all the classes in the school so that there is continuity and coherence in the children's experience? How to avoid repetition which dulls interest, and gaps which create excessive demand on understanding?

First it is necessary to explore the school's surroundings, keeping in mind the desired opportunities for learning. This means going out and walking round, perhaps sketching and making notes to describe the places and objects to be found. Note the opportunities for field work where observation and investigative work is possible and rewarding. Which sites, places or situations offer a challenge? What can children do there? For what purpose and by what means? Is it within a reasonable walking distance from the school? Does it offer opportunities for the sort of field work within the capacities of your children? The places or objects may be mainly related to living things, but they can also be chosen for physical characteristics or their technological nature.

Such a survey of the neighbourhood is best carried out by all the teachers in the school working together. Perhaps the area can be divided among them and a document produced, which constitutes a 'profile' of the potential of the neighbourhood. This profile will have to be updated regularly, which can be the role of the science co-ordinator, but it is very beneficial to compose the initial version together.

The second step is to develop outline individual class programmes which match particular studies to the changing capacities of the children. Clearly, this is also a matter which is best considered by the school staff as a whole. It may help to make distinctions between broad interests, for instance plants, 'minibeasts', communities, the soil and rocks. Whatever divisions are chosen should be decided by the whole team, bearing in mind the need to cover what is indicated in the Programmes of Study (DES, 1989) in a balanced and progressive manner. It may be helpful, for example, for one class to explore 'some way in which plant behaviour and life cycles are influenced by environmental conditions', leaving the similar exploration of focusing on animals for another class; alternatively, the division may be in terms of the context of study (minifield, transect or larger area) of both plants and animal behaviour.

Once these overall divisions had been made it is up to each teacher, each member of the team, to work out the details for his or her own class.

The next step, therefore, is to come down to concrete details in creating a class plan of work. This must be guided by the actual materials and equipment which are available and the possibilities offered by the environment as indicated in the 'profile'. Within this framework the plan should be quite specific about topics and the types of animals and plants, or other objects, which are to be studied. The methods of working should also be indicated.

If all this sounds rather too tightly controlled, it should perhaps be said that we are planning to set up an encounter. The plan is necessary to bring children and objects together, but once this has happened there must be plenty of room for spontaneity and pursuing activities arising from interests created in the children. We shall return to this matter later when considering practice.

Resources

Equipment

Reference has already been made to materials and equipment, the real and concrete objects that children explore or the ones they use in their exploration. The objects that they explore are in the environment or are taken (with care and only after thought about the effects of collection) from the environment to the classroom. They are of the kind mentioned on p. 43.

Materials and equipment used in exploration can be grouped in terms of their sources:

(1) those which are easily available and can be collected, often with the help of the children and their parents, e.g. jamjars, empty pots, pieces of wood,

potatoes, plastic bags, cardboard boxes, medicine bottles, squeezy bottles, and tins or plastic containers of many shapes and sizes;
(2) those which may already be available in school, e.g. rulers, pencils, pens, inks, colours, paints, brushes, scissors, tape, paper, glue, chalk;
(3) consumed materials which have to be bought but can be purchased easily and cheaply, e.g. plastic bags, salt, wire, string, bird seed, garden seeds, vinegar, soap, sand, candles, batteries;
(4) rather more sophisticated and permanent implements for which some school funds may be invested, e.g. hand lenses, measuring instruments such as graduated cylinders, a good balance, a micrometer, beakers, petri dishes and test tubes, an aquarium, tools and even a (stereo) microscope;
(5) pieces of apparatus which are too expensive to buy but can still probably be borrowed, e.g. a more sophisticated microscope from a nearby laboratory or school or teachers' centre; a lightmeter from a photographer, a bicycle belonging to a child, or a chicken from the farmer.

Sources of information

In the encounter, children 'ask the things themselves' to find the answers to their questions. Many questions will be answered this way; others will remain unanswered – which is not a bad thing since it leaves something to continue working on. Not all questions can be answered at first hand, partly because of time and partly because of the nature of the question. There is nothing against using other ways of finding out. One obvious way is to ask somebody who has already 'asked the things themselves', consulting them not out of laziness but from a genuine desire to understand better when one has gone as far as one can with one's own efforts.

People who have the relevant knowledge or expertise can sometimes be visited or invited to the school. More often, however, they are consulted through their books. The use of such sources of information as books, pictures, tapes, disks, etc., are aims of science education in their own right (see Attainment Targets 1 and 12 of the National Curriculum), as well as leading to an advance in understanding of the subject matter.

For these reasons it is important to provide materials for children to refer to, to read, to peruse, to browse through, to consult, to compare, to look at, to scrutinize, to talk about, to get explanation from, to be enlightened by, to illustrate, to summarize. The school should establish a smooth policy of purchasing and otherwise obtaining sound, suitable and reliable works and materials for reference, study and stimulation of further activity.

It bears repetition that these things, especially books, should not take the children away from working with real objects but should encourage them to do so. Books and pictures should link up with the children's investigations, should complement them, make the impossible possible, make present what is normally absent or too difficult to reach, bring near what is far away, connect what is related, and clarify what is misty and vague, so that the children, instead of being fobbed off with high-sounding words, return to their plants and animals, or other things under investigation, enriched with fresh ideas. It requires some effort to search for good documentation and illustrations, to sustain a consistently sound purchasing policy and to be prepared to prune from the school's bookshelves all that is obsolete. The school is not, of course, alone in its search for these resources. Help is generally available from library services, from museums, from teaching centres, advisory support and higher education institutions.

Resources for teachers

Bearing the responsibility for promoting the growth of knowledge and ability in the children brings with it the responsibility for one's own ability to accomplish this. Competence to teach does not come all at once; it takes experience and an accumulation of useful sources of information. Most successful teachers surround themselves with an assortment of books, booklets, cuttings from magazines and newspapers, lists of addresses and sympathetic contacts; they pick up free leaflets at exhibitions and always have an eye for something useful among the variety of circulars which reach the school or home. A school could well bring together and organize such information collected by individual teachers and make it available for showing.

It shouldn't be forgotten that the greatest resource is the environment itself. Thus we come back to the point, made on p. 61, that becoming familiar with the environment and helping to create a 'profile' of it is the best way to make full use of the greatest resource of all.

Classroom Practice

A well thought out plan of work, a knowledge of the parts of the outside world to be studied and the effort to provide appropriate materials lay the foundation for effective environmental science education. But much further thought has to be given to the details in organizing the work and the principles guiding the teacher's interaction with the children. Discussion in earlier chapters has hinted at approaches to these matters, so here we briefly bring these points together in a summary form.

(1) Generally, an open-ended learning situation should prevail in environ-

mental science education. To avoid misunderstanding on this it is recognized that there will always be times when clear, direct, instructions are to be given without further ado, in order to save time, to avoid danger, or to guarantee a good start to work. Very often these 'listen-to-me-carefully' instructions throw a clarifying light upon what would otherwise remain obscure or hidden. However, in relation to the actual uses of the materials and the response to the children's interests emanating from this work, a predominantly open learning situation is advocated.

An open learning situation, therefore, by no means implies that the children can flutter about in all the directions they fancy, but it does mean that, in the course of their learning activity, they can follow a direction which at that moment appears to be the most relevant, even though this was not foreseen by the teacher. Consultation, discussion and mutual trust between children and teacher play an important role in this teaching, choosing and learning process.

(2) Plan the detail of work within the theme you are engaged upon, in terms of the available materials and resources. Don't be deterred by what you do not have, but make use of what you do have with regard to outside opportunities, books, time and people.

(3) Let the children work in groups. Sometimes children in groups are working, each on his or her own problem, but often assisting one another. Sometimes, however, they cooperate as a group to solve common problems, or to solve a problem which requires co-operation. The considerable benefits of group collaboration, in which ideas are argued and thinking is provoked, will emerge later if children have regular experience of being in groups and talking to each other about their work from an early stage.

(4) Whenever children are confronted with something new (things, equipment or a situation) they will always need some time to acquaint themselves with it, to gear up to it, to explore its more obvious properties and possibilities: what it looks or feels like, what it can do, how it behaves, and how it can be manipulated.

This is a necessary phase, a serious activity of free exploration from which the first real questions for investigation arise. So don't hurry it or think that the children will never do more than appear to 'mess about'!

(5) If you decide to begin an activity with a class discussion, which is a very good way to start, wait until after the children have made their acquaintance with the materials. The children will then know what they are talking about and can then become involved in what you might propose, or make their own suggestions.

(6) Have ready ideas and assignments for work, especially for getting started when children's own questions are still vague or being formed.

(7) Help the children to put questions into words, and to state problems understandably. Some teachers write assignment cards for children which always end with: ' . . . and now ask your own question'.

(8) Give the children plenty of time to accomplish their work, but let them know what the time limit is.

(9) Allow children the time to work out and arrange their findings before you ask for a report, and give warning beforehand that you want to discuss the state of affairs or progress with them.

(10) Discuss with the children how they could, or should, record the results of their investigations: in writing, in drawing, or in diagram form. Also, help them decide how they could present their findings to others. Make a poster? An exhibition? A contribution to a class-book? A picture? An individual effort, or a group activity?

(11) It is advisable to gather independently working groups together at fixed times for a class discussion: to report to one another, exchange ideas, show results, raise remaining problems and to deliberate, all together, how to move on and what to tackle next. Even though the teacher will already have a plan ready in mind the children should feel that they are involved in decisions, and this should actually be the case. Commitment and motivation follow from such involvement and sweep aside all 'undisciplined' behaviour.

Implementing these principles in science teaching is not, of course, independent of the rest of the curriculum. There can be consistency in the way of working across different subjects despite differences in content. When children have developed the skills of using the encounter with things as a source of learning (coupled with selective use of books and other sources of information) and of reporting and discussing their work centrally, these skills can be used in other subject areas as well as science. It follows that other subjects should also be planned so that the children work with greater autonomy and independence.

6
EVALUATING THE ENCOUNTER

By the time you reach this last chapter we hope you will have been doing some of the activities as well as reading about them. You will be asking the question: how well am I doing? Here we offer a way of answering this question, but, ironically, through posing questions for you to ask yourself. Hopefully this self-checklist will enable teachers, at all stages in experience in this type of work, to judge their progress.

In Chapter 4 we suggested check-lists for assessing the children's progress. Here we are concerned with the quality of the encounter rather than its learning contents. This evaluation of the experience should precede any assessment of children, since there is no point in seeing if children have developed ideas and skills for which there has been no relevant learning opportunity. It will also come as a consequence of assessing children. If progress is not as hoped for, then the first thought should not be to consider the child as unable or at fault in some way but, rather, to examine the provision made for him or her to engage productively with the surrounding objects: Was the 'subject matter' of interest? Were demands made at too high or too low a level? Did the social group context prevent a genuine 'encounter' for this child? And so on. Thus evaluation of opportunity to learn and assessment of learning taking place form a cycle; one always leads to the other.

The first list below takes up this theme, focusing on the children's activities, either in the field or in the classroom. It can be used not only for 'trouble-shooting', where particular children might be the object of attention, but as a routine check at any time when the teacher can take a moment or two to stand back and review the whole class.

Checking on the Encounter

Are the children (in classroom or field):

- working in identifiable small groups?

- talking about their work (not about other things) without distracting each other?
- actually handling, or closely observing real things?
- absorbed, busy, or otherwise indicating that their work is important to them?
- finding parts of the work to puzzle over?
- able to follow the instructions you gave them, either orally or as a work card?
- asking questions about *how* to do their work or about what they are working with and what they are finding out?
- using equipment effectively to aid their investigations?
- making decisions themselves about the next step (and not expecting you to do this)?
- (in the classroom) using sources of information effectively?
- actually using process skills: observing, predicting, hypothesizing, fair testing, records, etc?

The list need not stop here; you may well add to it. If the answer to any of these is 'no' then some action needs to be taken. It is obvious from the questions what that action may be. For example, if children are not using equipment effectively they may need to be shown how to use it; if they are not absorbed and busy, find out what is distracting them or what things *do* interest them.

Self-Checklist

The response to the discovery that some of the children are not engaging the objects of study as effectively as you would wish may well be to throw your own actions and behaviour into the spot-light. Below are some questions you may well ask yourself, plus a few comments about each one.

- Do you know precisely what each group is doing?
  The implication is not that you should have determined or controlled what they are doing but, rather, that you should be aware of the changes in direction that are being taken, if only for safety's sake and so that you can discuss and question productively. If the answer is 'no', then you may have been spending too long with one or two groups and not circulating enough.
- Have you provided sufficient materials and equipment?
  If children have to wait for a turn to use something or to study something the waiting time may well result in a lowering of interest and motivation. The solution is to provide more objects if possible but, if not possible, to organize the activities so that there is a greater variety of things going on and less demand on those objects that are in short supply.

- Is the equipment accessible to the children?
  To promote self-directed learning the materials must be easily available, without children having to come to you for permission or for access. The responsibility for replacing items in their proper places has to be borne by the children and some vigilance is necessary when children are new to this idea.
- Do you express your questions in operational terms, that is, as action questions relating to what the children are doing?
  It should become second nature to pose your questions as do-questions, so that the attention of the children remains with, or is drawn back to, their work and the things they are working with, instead of being distracted towards you, or what they think are your whims or wishes. This takes some practice and occasional soul-searching, for you will often forget and ask an unintended why-question. However, as long as you are conscious of this danger, you can always detect and correct your mistake on the spot (see p. 17).
- Do you respond to children's questions in operational terms, that is, do you suggest what action they may take?
  Following on from the last point, you should try to respond 'operationally' to the questions your children ask while they are working. It is so easy to blurt out some ready-made answer which effectively stops the children searching. Of course, a little information given in a measured dose may often be of great relevance in the course of an investigation, if only to help the children over some hurdle, but the answers must encourage and not terminate their own searching (see p. 46).
- Do your interventions have a positive or negative effect on a group's working?
  You can judge this by observing from a distance the level of activity after you have left a group. (It is easier, however, for someone else to judge this – see later.) A 'monitoring' visit to the groups is important for keeping track of what they are doing, but this does not necessarily mean an interruption. By listening and observing unobtrusively it should be possible to pick out those moments when a brief discussion or a leading question is appropriate to stimulate the children's activity or to bring them back to the focus of the investigation.
- Do you talk too much?
  In both whole-class and small-group discussions try to resist dominating the scene. Invite the children to respond to each other rather than always being addressed by you. What you say should also encourage children to return to the materials, to 'ask the . . .' It should not run ahead of their experiences with real things and certainly not replace them. What you say

should relate to what has already been done and learned, helping to link it to further active encounters.

- Do you know enough about the area or objects which are being studied? You will never know all there is to know about things in the environment, for this is endless. However, for your own confidence and to avoid the possibility of confusing the children, it is necessary to get to know the environment and to collect books and other materials what will add to your direct experience of it (see pp. 24 and 61).

- Do you become engaged with the same subject matter as the children? This is related to the last item but it is not concerned with the type of background knowledge necessary for planning. Rather, it is a matter of whether you share in the fascination of studying those particular objects with which the children are engaged – the snails, the distribution of grasses, the tracks of small animals, etc. By sharing you help to bring about the encounter between children and objects and you can show by your comments and questions an example of scientific skills and attitudes in action. We're not of course suggesting that the teacher 'takes over' the activity – this would be impossible anyway because of all the groups – but that he or she takes part in it rather than standing aloof and outside it.

Working as a Team

Although the above list is expressed as a self-check list for teachers, it is evident that some questions are more easily answered by an observer than by the teacher. Teachers can help each other by observing each others' science work, looking for agreed aspects of teacher or pupil behaviour and feeding back this information. The observer sees what is going on behind the teacher's back and also provides a different perspective on those interactions involving the teacher. When help is mutual there is no suspicion or anxiety about being observed. Teachers who have practised this have found it extremely useful to them, even though there is never enough spare time to do it very often.

Support in evaluation is an aspect of the team work which plays an important part in providing an effective learning environment (see p. 61). If not only plans but experiences are discussed openly and frankly, then self-evaluation is important in identifying aspects of work where help is required. It is frequently the case that teachers have found solutions to each other's problems, and sharing is of mutual benefit. Although each teacher has to work with his or her own class or group, the responsibility for continuity and continuous improvement in the curriculum is collective.

EPILOGUE

Reading about science education is an honourable pastime which is to be recommended, but which is limited in its effect. Teaching science in the primary school – educating children through the processes of science – demands much personal effort, dedication, application and devotion throughout, because perfection is never reached.

Building up and carrying out a sequence of learning activities in science can be a source of pride and pleasure but it requires a great deal of creativity and professional skill. The responsibility for this should not be taken lightly; it should be taken collectively by a school staff, ideally under the enthusiastic and experienced leadership of the science coordinator.

We want children to leave the primary school with a lively understanding of, and a fair insight into, the natural world to which they belong and to which they are expected to make a positive contribution. For this we must give them the opportunity to develop their own powers of reasoning and thinking, and so increase their abilities to solve problems in a scientific manner, in pace with the phases of their development.

This rhetoric becomes a realistic goal for our efforts in science education if we genuinely allow the children to puzzle and ponder, to uncover and discover, to fail and to collect, to think about, to experiment with and to conclude about everything that their own surroundings, including the school, contain and offer.

REFERENCES

DES (1989) *Science in the National Curriculum*, HMSO, London.

Elstgeest, J. (1985) Encounter, interaction and dialogue, in W. Harlen (ed.) *Primary Science: Taking the Plunge*, Heinemann, London, pp. 9–20.

Elstgeest, J. (1985a) The right question at the right time, in W. Harlen (ed.) *Primary Science: Taking the plunge*, Heinemann, London, pp. 36–46.

Elstgeest, M. (1973) Dennis Dungball, in Outlook, *Journal of Environmental Education*, No. IX, p.e. Autumn Mountain View Centre for Environmental Education, University of Colorado, Denver, USA.

Harlen, W. (1983) *Guides to Assessment: Science*, Macmillan, London.

Jelly, S. (1985) Helping children raise questions – and answering them, in W. Harlen (ed.) *Primary Science: Taking the Plunge*, Heinemann, London, pp. 47–57.

Smith, D. (1988) *Industry Education in the Primary School Curriculum*, Falmer, London.

FURTHER READING

ASE and Nature Conservancy Council (1990) *Opening Doors for Science: some aspects of environmental education and science in the National Curriculum for 5 to 16*, Association for Science Education, Hatfield.

DES (1989) *Environmental Education from 5 to 16*, Curriculum Matters, HMSO, London.

Harlen, W. and Jelly, S. (1989) *Developing Science in the Primary Classroom*, Oliver and Boyd, Edinburgh.

Science 5/13 *Minibeasts (Stages 1 & 2), Trees (Stages 1 & 2, Using the Environment: Early Explorations; Investigations (Parts 1 and 2); Tackling Problems (Parts 1 and 2); Ways and Means*, Macdonald Education, London, 1974.

USEFUL ADDRESSES

Association for Science Education, College Lane, Hatfield, Herts AL10 9AA.

BP Educational Service, PO Box 5, Wetherby, W. Yorks LS23 7EH.

BP Film Library, 15, Beaconsfield Road, London NW10 2LE.

British Association for Young Scientists, Fortress House, 23 Saville Row, London W1X 1AB.

Countryside Commission, John Dover House, Crescent Place, Cheltenham, Gloucestershire GL50 3RA.

Philip Harris (science equipment), Lynn Lane, Shenstone, Staffordshire WS14 0EE.

Health Education Council, 78 New Oxford Street, London WC1A 1AH.

Meteorological Office, London Road, Bracknell, Berks, RG12 2SZ.

National Dairy Council, National Dairy Centre, John Princes Street, London W1M 0AP.

National Heritage, 9a North Street, London SW4.

Nature Conservancy Council, 19–20 Belgrave Square, London SW1X 5PY.

Osmiroid International Ltd (science equipment), Fareham Road, Gosport, Hampshire PO13 0AL.

Royal Society for Nature Conservation, The Green Nettleham, Lincoln LN2 2NR.

Royal Society for the Protection of Birds, The Lodge, Sandy, Bedfordshire SG19 2DL.

The School Natural Science Society, 22 Chada Avenue, Gillingham, Kent.

The Tree Council, 35 Belgrave Square, London SW1X 8QN.

WATCH (Junior Section of the Nature Conservation Trust), The Green, Nettleham, Lincoln LN2 2NR.

The Wildfowl Trust, Slimbridge, Gloucestershire GL2 7BT.

World Wildlife Fund, Education Project, Greenfield House, Guiting Power, Gloucestershire, GL54 5TZ.

Index